W9-BMF-376

STORIES OF JESUS

TOLD BY THEA HEINEMANN

Illustrated by Don Bolognese
Designed by Walter Brooks

A WHITMAN BOOK
Western Publishing Company, Inc.
Racine, Wisconsin

contents

Copyright © 1956, 1968 by WESTERN PUBLISHING COMPANY, INC.
PRODUCED IN U.S.A.
Library of Congress Catalog Card Number: 68-11122

WHITMAN is a registered trademark of Western Publishing Company, Inc.

STORIES
OF JESUS

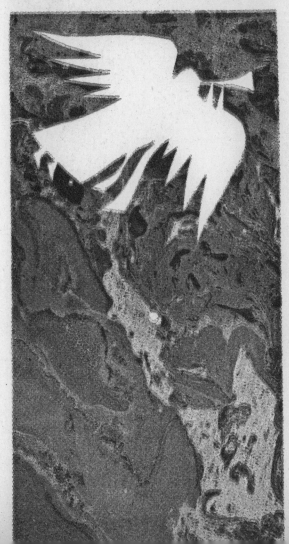

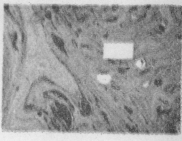

the
PROMISED SON

God made a promise to the people of the world. Everyone knows that when God makes a promise He keeps it. He promised to send His own Son into the world to be a Saviour to His people.

God chose a young maiden named Mary to be the mother of the Son of God. Mary kept the secret in her heart as long as she could. She felt humble but happy that God had chosen her to have the precious Babe.

Very soon the Christ Child was to be born. Mary hoped she could stay at her home, but God had said the Babe was to be born in Bethlehem. So He made the king of the land issue a decree. The King ordered everyone to register in the town from which his people had come. So Mary had to go to Bethlehem with her husband, Joseph.

They had to travel with a little donkey, and they put their supplies on its back. Mary rode on the animal's back, also, and Joseph walked.

As they went along, Mary and Joseph talked about the things

they saw. They saw the fields where their very own ancestor David had watched his flocks when he was a shepherd.

They saw a mother holding a tiny baby close to her. Mary sighed happily. Soon she would have a tiny baby to cradle in her arms. Her baby would be the Holy Christ Child.

Mary and Joseph went around a bend in the road and left the village behind. They came upon another little town. As they traveled all day, they passed another, and another. This was no lonely road. There were towns all along the way.

The journey was nearly ended. There were many people on the road now. They were travelers, too. They were going to Bethlehem for the same reason that took Mary and Joseph. Some were walking. Some were riding burros. All had bundles of belongings. All would be looking for a place to stay in the town that night.

"Look up the hill!" exclaimed Joseph. "See the lights ahead? We are almost there!"

Clippety-clop! Clippety-clop! The little donkey's hoofbeats sounded loud on the rough road.

They entered the town. It was crowded with people. Where would Mary and Joseph find a room for the night?

If Joseph was worried, he did not let Mary know it. He inquired at a number of places. Each time he was turned away. There was no room for them.

At last he came to an innkeeper.

"Have you any place where my wife may rest for the night?" he asked.

The man looked at the anxious husband. He saw Mary, his

wife, huddled uncomfortably on the donkey's back. She looked so weary and worn.

"There is only a place in the stable," said the man. "If you wish, you may go there."

In the side of a hill there was a cave of rock which was sometimes used as a shelter for animals. Joseph led Mary to this place.

He made a comfortable bed where she could rest. It was quiet away from the great crowds of people.

Mary was glad to be here in this lowly place.

In the night, the precious Christ Child was born to Mary. God fulfilled His promise. He sent His beloved Son Jesus into the world. As a tiny baby He came.

Mary took long strips of cloth which she wrapped tenderly around the dear Baby. These were His swaddling clothes. They were the clothes of a newborn child of the land, in those long-ago days.

In a lowly manger lay the tiny Baby, the promised Son of God. He was not born in a fine palace. He had no need of a palace for His home. The Christ Child did not need great people to care for Him. He was surrounded by something far more precious. He had the love of His mother, Mary, and the devoted care of Joseph.

The night He was born, God sent His angels from heaven. They appeared in the sky and sang a song of great joy, telling the good news of the Christ Child's birth. God had kept His promise. He had sent His Son to be the Saviour of the world.

the song
of the angels

It was the middle of the night. The streets of the little town of Bethlehem were empty. Houses were dark, except for the small light that always burned in every Israelite home. Almost all the people were fast asleep.

In the fields near Bethlehem there were some men who were not sleeping. They were shepherds who watched their sheep at night.

The shepherds looked up at the clear night sky. They saw the twinkling stars.

Suddenly a bright light burst in the sky. An angel of the Lord appeared before their very eyes.

The angel knew the men were frightened. He said, "Fear not. I have Good News. It will bring joy to all people. In Bethlehem you will find a baby wrapped in swaddling clothes, lying in a manger. He is Christ, the Lord, the Saviour of the world."

All heaven became bright with a great light. The angel was not alone. He was surrounded by many angels. Together they sang a beautiful song. We know the words of that song because we find them written in the Bible.

This was the song:

"Glory to God in the highest, and on earth peace, goodwill toward men!"

The bright light in the sky faded. The angels went away into heaven. The earth was once more in the shadow of the night.

The shepherds blinked their eyes. They looked at one another and began asking questions.

"Did you see the angels?" asked one.

"Did you hear them singing?" asked another.

"The first angel had a message," cried another shepherd. "The Saviour is born! We will find Him in Bethlehem."

"The angel said He would be wrapped in swaddling clothes, lying in a manger. Let us go now and find Him!"

The shepherds left the hills. In the dark night they climbed the road that led to Bethlehem.

The town was still fast asleep. No one could be seen on the streets. Houses were still dark, except for the ever-present tiny flickering lights in the Israelite homes.

The angel said the Lord was born in Bethlehem. The shep-

herds knew then that they must find the new Babe somewhere in the town. They knew they must find the blessed Babe that very night.

At last they found the place where Mary and Joseph were staying. When the shepherds asked about the Christ Child, they learned that a new baby boy had been born in this very place.

"Is He lying in a manger, wrapped in swaddling clothes?" asked the shepherds.

When Joseph said yes, the shepherds knew they had found the Christ Child about whom the angels had sung their song.

The shepherds crowded into the room. They wanted to see the new Baby.

"We were watching the sheep on the hillside," explained one of the men. "All of a sudden a great light shone in the sky. An angel appeared and told us that Christ the Lord was born."

"We were very frightened!" exclaimed another shepherd.

"But the angel told us not to be afraid," said the first man.

Joseph and Mary looked at the shepherds as they stood adoring the new Baby. They listened with wonder to their story.

The shepherds told about the angel choir, singing praises in heaven because the Christ Child was born. Never before, in all the world, had anything like this happened.

The shepherds gazed upon the tiny Christ Child in adoration. Joseph looked at the precious Babe as Mary, the mother, lifted the Little One and held Him close in her arms.

He was God's Son. Here was the Saviour of the world. God had promised to send a Saviour to His people. He had kept His word.

The shepherds finally said good-bye. They went back to their flocks on the hillside.

Everywhere they went, they talked about the great vision in the night. They told of the angels singing to the glory of God. They told about the birth of the Saviour.

Sometime later, the shepherds took their sheep to the Temple in Jerusalem. They met many people gathered in the Temple court. To all, they told the Good News. God had sent His Son into the world. God's own angels had appeared in the sky to tell the Good News.

Mary and Joseph stayed in Bethlehem, caring for the Child. They, too, often spoke of the wonder of the angels' appearance in the sky. They remembered the words of the only song that was ever sung in all the world by angels in heaven.

"Glory to God in the highest, and on earth peace, goodwill toward men!"

a Day
of thanksgiving

When you receive a nice gift, you want to give thanks for it.

A new baby in a home is a very nice gift from God. When the mother and father look at the tiny baby, they are filled with joy. They say, "Thank you, Heavenly Father, for sending the gift of a healthy child to our home."

Mary and Joseph were very happy when God sent His Son as a baby to their home. Each day the Baby became more precious to Mary. Her heart was very joyful. She wanted to give thanks to God.

Mary counted the days from His birth.

"Today my Son is twelve days old," she said.

Another time she said, "Jesus is twenty days old."

Then one day Joseph said, "Tomorrow the Christ Child will be forty days old."

"It is the day we have long awaited!" exclaimed Mary happily. "Tomorrow we can take Him to the Temple in Jerusalem. We can give thanks to God for the great gift of His Son."

Very, very early the next morning, Mary and Joseph left the little town of Bethlehem, where they had been living. They had about six miles to travel before they reached the Temple. Mary

and Joseph wanted to be there when the Temple gates were opened.

Shops in the town were not open. The streets were empty. Most everybody was sleeping when Mary and Joseph started their journey.

The sky was blue-gray. Slowly it changed to shades of pink. A big orange-red ball appeared in the eastern sky. Clouds changed their shapes. The ball became larger and brighter until it was very bright and its rays shone over all the earth.

A new day had begun.

The sun's appearance in the sky told of a new and very special day. It was the day that Mary and Joseph brought the Christ Child to the Temple, to give thanks for Him.

As they neared Jerusalem they could hear three trumpet blasts.

"They are opening the outer gate of the Temple," said Joseph.

"Let us hurry," said Mary. "We want to be there early."

"We want to follow the custom of our people," said Joseph as they reached the outer gate. "We are from the tribe of Israel. It is on the fortieth day that we are to present the Baby to the priest and give thanks for Him."

"Let us take a thanksgiving offering," said Mary. "There are some men selling doves. Let us buy two of them."

Joseph opened the strings of his purse. He reached in and drew out the money to pay for the doves that were to be their offering to God.

While Mary and Joseph were in the Temple worshiping God,

an old, old man came toward them. He looked at the Christ Child. A bright smile came to his face. He reached out his arms to hold the Infant close to him.

Mary looked at the old man. His name was Simeon. He was well known at the Temple, for he came every day to praise God and talk to Him in prayer. Daily he read words from God which were written on long scrolls. These words were the same that you have in your own Bible today.

Simeon had read about Jesus. He knew that God was sending His Son to be the Saviour of the world. Simeon's one great wish in all his life was to live to see the Messiah, God's Son.

When Simeon saw Mary holding the tiny Baby in her arms, God let him know that this was the promised Jesus. After years and years of waiting, Simeon had, at last, seen the Saviour.

He took the Baby from Mary's arms.

He thanked God and said, "My eyes have seen the salvation which You have prepared before the face of all people. It is a light to lighten the Gentiles and the glory of the people of Israel."

Mary listened with wonder to the words of old Simeon. He knew that Jesus was the Son of God!

More people were coming into the Temple at this time. There were many who came every day to praise and thank God.

Slowly an old woman named Anna came toward them. Like Simeon, she had come to the Temple each day for many years to praise God and thank Him.

Anna knew that God had promised to send a Saviour to His people. When she saw the Baby Jesus, in the arms of Mary, God

let Anna know that He was the promised Christ. Anna was filled with joy and thanksgiving to God.

It was a day of much rejoicing and giving of thanks.

Mary and Joseph had come to the Temple to thank God for His gift of the Christ Child to their home. Simeon had seen the Saviour, after many long years of waiting. He gave thanks to God. Anna, the faithful worshiper, rejoiced and gave thanks that her dim old eyes had looked upon the fair Child.

Mary and Joseph returned with the Baby Jesus to their home in Bethlehem.

God had looked with favor on their home. He had entrusted to their care, His own Son. Mary and Joseph could show how thankful they were by guarding and keeping well the wonderful gift of the Christ Child.

the visit
of the wise men

Many travelers entered the gates to the city of Jerusalem. Sometimes they wore clothes that were very different from those of the people who lived there. These were travelers from far-away countries. The people who lived in the city of Jerusalem looked at them and wondered about their homelands.

King Herod lived in Jerusalem. He had a beautiful palace for his home. He was very old. He was not a good man. Many people came to visit King Herod from distant lands. Sometimes they brought priceless gifts to the king. These were not love gifts. They were given to win his favor. Many people were afraid of Herod.

One day some travelers came to the gates of Jerusalem. They entered the city. They went through the streets. They wore different clothes. People turned around in the streets to look at them. They wondered why they had come and who they were.

The strangers began asking questions.

"Do you know where we can find the newborn King of the Jews?" they asked.

People shook their heads to say no. Everybody in Jerusalem knew that there was only one ruler. He was the old and wicked King Herod.

The strangers had more to say. "We saw His star in the East. We have traveled many miles to worship Him. We have been on the road for many days."

This was news to all who heard it. People stopped on street corners to talk about the strangers. Who were they? Where was the newborn king they were seeking? What would happen when King Herod heard of another who was claimed to be a ruler?

The people of Jerusalem trembled with fear, for they knew their king would be angry.

News of the strange visitors reached the palace. Herod was filled with anger. He was the king! No man was going to take his place.

King Herod called his men to the throne room. He asked them many questions. Who were these travelers? Where was the newborn king they were seeking?

The king's men told him what they knew.

"They are Wise Men who have come from the East," they said.

"These strangers saw a light in the sky. It foretold the birth of a new king. They have come to worship him. They have brought fine gifts with them," said one of the men.

Herod was more angry than ever. Fine gifts were for him! They were not to be given to a baby who was said to be a new king.

Herod's men were almost afraid to tell the other news that they had heard in the city.

"There is much talk among the people about a newborn king," said one man. "The Israelites have long been waiting for a Messiah to be born. Many say God has sent His Son to be the Saviour of the world."

"What do the scrolls in the Temple say?" demanded the king.

"They foretell the birth of the Christ Child. The prophets say He will be born in Bethlehem."

"We have heard other news," said one of the king's men. "A Baby was brought to the Temple. He was born in Bethlehem. His name is Jesus. When Simeon and Anna saw the Baby, they both declared He was the promised Saviour."

There was more news for the king. "Shepherds from the fields near Bethlehem brought their sheep to the Temple. They told a strange story. They said the sky was suddenly bright one night.

An angel appeared and told them to find the Christ Child in Bethlehem. Then a choir of angels sang in heaven, declaring the glory of the Child's birth."

"So, the new king is in Bethlehem!" cried Herod angrily. "I am the king! As long as I live, I will be the ruler over all this land. No one will take my place!"

Then Herod gave an order that the Wise Men were to be brought before him.

When they came, they answered all the questions that the king asked them. They told the same story he had heard from his own men. They had seen a strange star in the sky. They had followed it. They were seeking a newborn king in Bethlehem. They had stopped at Jerusalem to ask about the baby. This was a busy city. They thought that somebody would have heard the Good News and could tell them about the birth of the Messiah.

The king was very crafty. He did not let the Wise Men know he was angry. He did not let them know he had some bad plans and that he wanted to use them to help carry out his wicked ideas.

He said to the Wise Men, "Go to Bethlehem. If you find the king, let me know. I want to worship him, also."

The Wise Men left the king's palace. They traveled the road that led to Bethlehem. They looked in the sky. They saw the bright star shining again. It was leading the way to the place where the Christ Child stayed.

The Wise Men found the little home where Mary and Joseph lived. They found the Christ Child there.

Many miles they had traveled in search of the Baby. All along the way, a star had led them until it hovered over this humble place.

The Wise Men bowed down and worshiped the Christ Child. They presented their fine gifts of gold, frankincense, and myrrh for the Baby Jesus, who was born to be the Saviour of the world.

When they had visited for a while, the Wise Men returned to their homes in a faraway land. They did not go back to Jerusalem to the wicked King Herod's palace. God told them in a dream that they must not tell the king of their visit to the Christ Child.

God was watching over His beloved Son.

Herod could be ruler in his palace in Jerusalem. He could rule his land until he died.

Jesus was born to be a ruler of all who would love and serve Him in the world. Jesus was the everlasting King!

the Flight into egypt

King Herod sat waiting in his palace. He did not like to wait. When he gave orders, he expected them to be obeyed. If people disobeyed him, he became very angry.

King Herod had waited many days for the Wise Men to return to his palace. But they had not come. He had given orders to them. They had not obeyed his command.

Finally Herod realized that the Wise Men had disobeyed his orders. He must send his own men to Bethlehem to find the baby who was proclaimed to be the newborn king.

Jesus was the baby that King Herod was seeking. Jesus was God's own Son.

God knew about the wicked Herod. He knew that the king had ordered his men to search all Bethlehem for any baby boys they could find, hoping to capture the One about whom the Wise Men talked.

Before Herod's men arrived, an angel came to Joseph while he was sleeping and said, "Arise and take the young Child and His mother and flee into Egypt. Stay there until I tell you, for Herod will seek the Child to destroy Him."

Joseph woke Mary. He told her of the angel's warning.

"We must leave this very night," he said.

"God has been with us," said Mary. "He will lead us safely to Egypt."

Quickly, Joseph and Mary packed their belongings. They took the presents the Wise Men had brought to Jesus. They were glad to have the gold. It helped buy supplies for their journey.

Throughout the night Joseph and Mary traveled with the dear Christ Child. They were tired and anxious to rest, but they knew that they could not stop until they were far away from King Herod's men.

God was watching over the little family. He did not let King Herod's men find them.

They traveled many days.

The trip through the desert was long and tiresome. Joseph had bought food. He had packed leather bottles filled with water. These supplies had to last them through the sandy desert journey.

The hot sun shone on the bright sand. It was not easy to urge their little donkey to walk through the shifting sand.

At night it was cooler, but it was dry and dusty. Little clouds of sand and dust circled around the family when they camped at night.

At last they came to a place in Egypt in which many of their people lived. Here they found a place to stay while they waited for God's angel to tell them they could return to their homeland.

Mary and Joseph did not have to stay in Egypt very long. In a few months God sent His angel to tell Joseph that he could go home. King Herod was dead.

Joseph had planned to return to Bethlehem. When he heard that the new ruler over that town was a wicked man, he decided to take his family to Nazareth instead. They would be safe there.

Across the hot desert sand they traveled again. They journeyed for many days until they came to Nazareth.

Happily, Joseph and Mary settled there with the blessed Christ Child.

It was good to be at home again. It was good to bring to their home the Baby Jesus. There He could live and grow to be a healthy boy.

the child
Jesus at home

Have you ever wondered what it was like to be a child at the time when Jesus was on earth?

There is not very much to be read in the Bible about the childhood of Jesus. We do know how other people lived in those days, and from this we can guess much about the Saviour's life.

Let us go back, then, to the small town of Nazareth in the faraway land of Palestine. Let us visit the house where Jesus lived in the days of His childhood.

There was one big room in Jesus' house. Here the family ate their meals and slept. All their belongings were here. The room was crowded with things that they needed for daily living.

Large pottery jars stood by the door. Jesus knew His mother stored food in some of these. Other jars were used for water.

Joseph had made some shelves in a corner of the room. These were used for storing many of the family's belongings.

There was a low table where they ate their meals. Mother Mary had made cushions, and at mealtime each member of the family sat on a cushion by the small table. When company came, they sat on the cushions to be comfortable while visiting.

There were mats rolled neatly and placed against the wall. Every evening the mats were unrolled and spread on the floor. These were the beds for the family.

There was a loom where Mary wove material to make clothes for her family. The pots and spoons she needed for cooking hung on the walls. Even the ceiling was used for storage. Large rings of onions, herbs, garlic, and dried raisins hung from the rafters.

Everything the family needed was gathered together in this one room which was their home.

When Jesus was a child He often watched His mother prepare the meal for her family. There were no gas or electric stoves in those days. Mary had to build a fire in the yard to cook the food. Before she could build the fire, she needed fuel. So Jesus learned where to find brushwood. When He was quite small, His mother went with Him. She filled His arms with brushwood and carried a large bundle herself. When He was older, Jesus learned to go alone.

Mary baked bread for the family. She needed water for the dough. She took her young Son by the hand and led Him down

the street to the well. She drew water and poured it into her water jar. She placed the jar on her head and balanced it there with one hand, while she held her Son's hand with the other. Together they walked home.

By and by, Jesus learned the way to the well. He was able to go there alone. Then His mother gave Him a jar and He drew water from the well and brought it to the house.

Jesus watched His mother as she cut vegetables for a big stew. She poured water in a pot with the vegetables and put them over the fire to cook. The smell of the food was good. Little Jesus hopped and skipped around the yard, waiting to taste the stew.

He was glad when His mother said it was time to eat. Like all boys, He was always hungry.

The little family gathered around the low table in the house, and a prayer was said to God. In the center of the table stood the big bowl of stew. Mary passed bread to everyone. She took some for Jesus and some for herself. She folded her bread and dipped it into the pot of stew. Then she ate the bread and stew together.

Mary guided the little hands of Jesus to fold His bread and dip it into the stew and eat it.

Afterward, Mary brought a pitcher of water and a towel. She poured water on the hands of those at the table. Each person dried his hands with the towel. A prayer of thanks was said and the meal was over.

Mary was always busy. Jesus watched as she wove material for the clothes the family wore.

In those days a family did not have many changes of clothing. Each one had an outfit which he wore almost all the time.

A man or a boy wore much the same kind of dress that a woman wore. Everyone wore a shirt that came to the knees. It had no sleeves and it was held together by a sash at the waist. Over this was worn a coat, a long one for a woman and a shorter one for a man.

Some coats were striped or made of bright-colored material. There was a girdle or sash worn at the waist, to hold the coat together. The big key to the house was sometimes tied to the girdle. A man carried his money pouch there.

Jesus was proud to wear His coat. His mother had spent many hours making it for Him. When He was quite small, she had to help Him with the girdle, but He soon learned to help Himself.

There was much that the Christ Child had to learn as He grew up in the little house in Nazareth. He needed the help of His mother.

Gladly she taught Him. Proudly she watched Him grow. She was glad that He found favor with the people in their town, for everyone knew that Jesus was a good child.

God, the Heavenly Father, looked down upon the Child Jesus in Nazareth and He was pleased.

A man named Luke wrote about the young boy. In a few words he told about the Christ Child growing up in His simple, happy home.

He said it like this: "Jesus increased in wisdom and stature and in favor with God and man."

jesus at school

Jesus stayed home when He was a very small child. When He was about six years old, He started to school in the busy little town of Nazareth.

In those times school was quite different from school that boys and girls attend today. In the first place, only the boys were able to go. The girls stayed at home with their mothers.

Lessons were taught in the church, called a synagogue. The teacher sat on a stool and the little boys sat crosslegged on the floor. The teacher had a long scroll from which he read to his pupils. The lessons that the boys learned were from the part of God's Book that we call the Old Testament.

When the teacher read a story from the scroll, the schoolboys knew he was talking about people who had lived long ago. They understood that these men and women who were heroes of the stories were ancestors of theirs. They knew that ancestors were relatives who lived many years before.

The teacher did not always read stories to his pupils. There were many beautiful verses that he taught them from the scrolls. The boys had to repeat the words after the teacher. Sometimes their heads swayed back and forth in rhythm with the verses as they chanted them.

There were very strict laws that the teacher taught the boys. These were laws given to the people by God, and they were to be obeyed.

Jesus learned to read with other pupils in the class. After a while He could take the scrolls which His teacher used, and read the writing there without any help.

Jesus learned to write, or print, in the language of His times.

Year after year Jesus went to the classroom. In that time He learned to know the stories from God's Book. He learned many verses that were written there. He learned to know the laws God wanted His people to obey. His mind was filled with the teachings from His Heavenly Father's Book.

Everywhere He went, Jesus felt God's Presence. At home His family always looked to God for loving care. In the fields and on the hills Jesus could see and feel God's loving care. In school He learned about God's love from His Sacred Book.

jesus
at the temple

When Jesus was twelve years old, He went with Mary and Joseph to celebrate His first Passover Feast.

The family had to leave their home in Nazareth and travel to the Temple in Jerusalem for the celebration.

This was the best time in the early life of the Child Jesus.

While they were in Jerusalem celebrating the Passover Feast, Jesus spent most of the time in the Temple. It was His Heavenly Father's House. He felt that He belonged there.

Jesus found some teachers sitting on the terrace of the great Temple. These men talked to anyone who came to them with questions about God.

Jesus stood nearby. He listened to the teachers. He went closer to the place where they sat. At last He was right beside them.

The teachers looked at the young Lad. They wondered about Him. They were surprised that He knew so much about God. They did not know that they were talking to God's own Son.

Days passed swiftly. It was time to return to Nazareth.

Mary and Joseph gathered together their belongings and started toward home. There were many families going their way. Mary and Joseph joined these people.

Some boys and girls were running and playing on the road, ahead of their parents. Some children lagged behind. There were so many people traveling that the parents did not know where to look for their sons and daughters.

Joseph and Mary were certain that Jesus would soon come running to them. But He did not come!

They were worried. They wondered what had happened to the Boy. They hurried from one family group to another.

"Have you seen Jesus?" they asked.

The answer was always, "No, we have not seen Jesus."

None of the children remembered seeing Him during the day's journey. Jesus was nowhere to be found!

There was nothing to do but to return to Jerusalem to search for the Child.

When they reached the city, Joseph and Mary hurried to the place where they had stayed. The people there shook their heads.

"No," they said, "we have not seen Jesus."

Three days passed and Joseph and Mary had not found Jesus. They had searched everywhere. They had stopped many people, asking if they had seen the Boy.

Always the answer was, "No, we have not seen Him."

There was one last place to look. It was the Temple.

Anxiously, Mary and Joseph went there. To their great relief they found Jesus talking to the great teachers He had met on the terrace of the Temple.

For days the Boy had been in this same place, asking questions and listening to the answers which the teachers told Him.

Jesus had forgotten completely to count the days and to remember that it was time to return home. He was so eager to learn all He could about His Heavenly Father that He forgot everything else.

Mary and Joseph were very glad to see the Boy after many days of searching for Him.

Mary said, "Son, why did You do this to us? We have looked everywhere for You and we were sorrowing over You."

Jesus looked at His Mother.

"Why did you worry about Me?" He asked. "Didn't you know that I would be here? There is so much I must learn about My Heavenly Father. This is My Father's House. These teachers have been telling Me much that I need to know."

Mary listened to her Son's words. He was right. Jesus was God's Son. He should learn all that He could while He was at the Temple, for the Temple was God's House.

Jesus said good-bye to His teachers. He left the Temple and went with Mary and Joseph.

The little family gathered together all of their belongings and traveled back to their home in Nazareth.

Jesus settled down in His home again, obeying His mother and helping Joseph with chores.

The celebration of the Passover Feast in Jerusalem was never forgotten by the little family.

Baptism of Jesus

One day Jesus left the town of Nazareth, where He lived. He walked twenty miles to a place on the River Jordan called Bethabara.

When He was near the river He saw many people gathered there. They were crowding around a certain man.

Jesus went closer. He wanted to hear what the stranger was saying.

"It is Good News I have to tell!" cried the stranger. "The Saviour is coming. Prepare for Him!"

"Who are you?" asked one of the men in the crowd.

"I am a voice crying in the wilderness," was the reply. "I am a messenger of the Good News. My name is John."

"What day will the Saviour come?" asked another listener.

"I do not know what day it will be," said John. "I only know He is coming. You must be ready. We have waited many long years for this day."

"Ah, yes," cried the people. "What must we do to be ready?"

"Be sorry for those things which you have done that are wrong," said John. "Ask God to forgive you. Try to do that which is pleasing to Him."

"We will!" cried the people, and they crowded around John.

After they had made this promise, the men and women came forward, one by one, and John baptized them in the waters of the Jordan River.

Jesus watched the people. Some were from towns. Others were farmers. There were traders and tax collectors. There were soldiers. All of them wanted to be ready for the Saviour's coming.

When all the people were baptized, Jesus walked to the place where John stood.

John looked at the young man who stood before him. At first, he did not know who it was. Suddenly he knew the One who stood there was Jesus, the Saviour!

John had long been waiting for the Saviour's coming. He had traveled up and down the River Jordan, telling people to be ready for Him. But when the Saviour came to him, John did not know what to do.

"You have come to me?" asked John humbly.

"It must be this way," said Jesus. "This is to fulfill God's plan."

Then John knew what he must do. He must baptize Jesus.

As the Saviour went up, out of the water, the heavens opened. A Vision like a dove lighted upon Jesus and a Voice was heard:

"This is My beloved Son, in whom I am well pleased."

These were words that Jesus always remembered. God was well pleased with His Son. Jesus knew He was ready now to begin His work as Saviour of the world.

jesus makes new friends

Jesus had been alone in the wild hill country for many days. He was ready now to be with friends and talk with them.

There was a friend who knew that Jesus was the Son of God. That man was John. Jesus walked down the hill to the River Jordan, where He knew He would find this friend.

There he was, by the river, talking with some fishermen.

John looked up. He saw Jesus coming toward him.

Excitedly he pointed in that direction and said to the fishermen, "There He is, the promised Saviour. I have been telling you about Him all this time."

The two fishermen looked at Jesus. They wanted to be closer to Him. They wanted to talk with Him. They started to walk toward Him.

When they approached, Jesus said, "What are you seeking?"

When He asked this question, the fishermen did not know how to answer. They wanted to be near Jesus. They wanted to talk with Him. They did not know how to tell this to the Saviour.

One of the men asked, "Master, where are You staying?"

"Come with Me and see," replied Jesus.

The two men were so happy that they could scarcely speak. The Messiah had invited them to be with Him! He wanted to talk with them.

The fishermen followed Jesus. Eagerly they listened to His words. It was good to be in His company.

It was night when they left Jesus. As the two friends walked under the starlit sky, they talked about their new Friend. They knew that forever after they would be happier for having found such a Friend.

One of the two men was named Andrew. He was so glad to know Jesus that he wanted to tell the news to someone else.

Andrew thought of his brother. "I must tell Simon I have found the Messiah."

Andrew hurried to his brother. He told him the good news.

Andrew led his brother Simon to the place where Jesus was staying. Jesus welcomed Andrew's brother.

He said, "I know who you are. I know all about you. They call you Simon. I am going to give you a new name. You shall one day be called Peter, which means the Rock. You shall earn this name, for you shall become strong like a rock."

Simon did not understand all that Jesus told him. He knew he wanted to be a friend to Jesus. That was enough for him.

Now there were three friends. There were the two fishermen and the brother named Simon. There were to be more loyal friends.

Jesus found one the next day. His name was Philip.

Jesus said to him, "Follow Me."

Philip was glad to go wherever Jesus went. It was a wonderful

thing to be chosen by the Messiah to be a friend. He felt very humble. He wanted to share his joy with someone he loved. He thought of his friend named Nathaniel.

He hurried to him. He found him sitting under a fig tree.

"A most wonderful thing has happened!" he exclaimed. "The Messiah has come! I have seen Him with my own eyes. He even chose me to follow Him."

Nathaniel did not say anything. He was thinking about this news. For hundreds of years people had hoped for the coming Messiah. It was hard to believe that He had come at last.

Philip was impatient with Nathaniel.

"You must see for yourself," he said. "Follow me."

Nathaniel went with Philip to Jesus.

As they came toward him Jesus looked at Nathaniel and said, "There is a good man."

Nathaniel looked at Jesus wonderingly. "How do You know who I am?" he asked.

"I know all about you," said Jesus. "Before your friend Philip found you under the fig tree, I knew about you."

Nathaniel bowed his head humbly. He said, "You are the Son of God."

"Do you say this because I knew about you?" asked Jesus. "Do you believe in Me, just because I knew that you were to be found under the fig tree? Greater things than this shall happen. You shall see angels coming down from heaven to the Son of Man."

Nathaniel looked up. He saw Jesus smiling at him with loving kindness.

"I want to be a friend of Jesus," he thought.

Gladly, Nathaniel joined the little group of friends. Now there were five. There were the two fishermen. There was Simon. There were the two friends, Philip and Nathaniel.

These friends followed Jesus wherever He went.

It was good to have Jesus for a Friend.

the
wedding at cana

The little village of Cana was buzzing with excitement. It was the day which a young maiden and a man of the village had chosen for their wedding.

That evening, friends and neighbors were all ready and waiting for the wedding procession to come down the street.

Some folks listened at their windows for the sound of the flute players and the songs of happy singers, which heralded the coming of the bride. Some friends went to the doors of their homes and peered down the street. They were watching for bright torches flaring in the dark and lighting the way.

Suddenly the whole street became bright with the light of the torches, and gay with happy songs. The wedding procession was on its way to the house of the groom!

In the procession walked the bride. She was dressed in a lovely gown. Over this she wore a long heavy veil. On her head was a wreath of myrtle leaves.

As the wedding party passed the houses of friends and neighbors, they, too, joined the happy group.

Many, many people had joined the procession by the time it reached the house of the groom.

It was here that the simple wedding ceremony was performed, by which the bride and groom became husband and wife.

It was a happy time for everyone.

The bride and groom were glad so many friends had come to wish them well. They were especially happy to know that Jesus, their good friend, had come to the wedding.

A big feast had been prepared for the guests. The groom was anxious to have enough food and wine for all the company. He had hired a man whom he called a governor to be in charge of the feast. This man was to keep a watchful eye on the table to see that there was plenty to eat and enough to drink.

It was not the governor who noticed that something was missing on the table. It was Mary, the mother of Jesus, who saw that there was no more wine. Something needed to be done about this. She knew there was no more wine in the house.

Mary hurried to the place where Jesus stood and whispered to Him, "They have no wine!"

Mary knew that her Son could be helpful to His friends.

There was a way that Jesus could help. He knew He had the Divine Power from God to provide wine for the wedding feast in a special way that no man could do it. Never before had He used this power from God to help other people.

The wedding guests knew Jesus was their kind friend and neighbor. They did not know that Jesus had been sent on earth by God to be their helper. They did not know He was God's own Son. They did not know He could help them in a very special way by performing miracles.

The time had come for Jesus to perform His first miracle and

to let His friends know He was sent by God to be their helper.

Jesus let His mother know He was ready to help His friends. There were servants standing nearby. Mary called to them. She said, "Whatever He tells you to do, do it."

Against the wall, near the door, were some water pots. Jesus pointed to these and said to the servants, "Fill the water pots with water."

The servants did not know why they should do this, but they obeyed the command of Jesus. They filled the water pots full to overflowing with water and brought them back to Jesus.

"Now draw from the water pots," said Jesus, "and take some to the governor of the feast."

The servants dipped into the water pots. They could not believe their own eyes. They drew rich sparkling red wine from the water pots, which they had just filled with water a few moments before.

The servants looked at Jesus in great wonder and amazement. He had turned water into wine!

One of the servants hurried with a small vessel of wine to the governor of the feast.

The governor took a taste of the wine. It was better than any

he had ever tasted before. He did not know of this miracle that Jesus had performed. He thought the servant brought some wine that had been put aside to be used later for the feast.

He hurried to the bridegroom and said, "Why do you leave the best until last? This wine that you just served is better than any I have ever tasted!"

The bridegroom did not understand how such a thing could happen.

"Where did you get this?" he asked.

"The servant brought it to me," explained the governor of the feast.

The servant was called.

"Where did you get this wine?" the bridegroom asked the servant.

"It came from the water pots by the doorway," replied the servant.

"The water pots hold water, not wine!" exclaimed the bridegroom.

Excitedly the servant told the bridegroom what had happened. He told of filling the water pots with water. He told of drawing the rich wine from the same water pots, at the command of Jesus.

This was a miracle!

The news spread. Soon the friends of Jesus knew He had performed a strange miracle. He had turned water into wine!

This was the first time Jesus showed His Divine Power from God. This was only the beginning of many, many miracles which Jesus performed to help those who needed Him.

GOOD NEWS FOR
A POOR RICH MAN

All over the land the news was spreading about Jesus. Many people had seen Him at the Temple in Jerusalem during the Passover Feast. They had heard Him preach. They had seen the wonderful miracles He performed.

As they traveled homeward, the people spread the good news. When they reached home, they told neighbors and friends about Jesus.

The good news reached the city of Capernaum. At the wharf, by the Sea of Galilee, the fishermen talked as they cleaned their nets and washed their boats.

There was an old fisherman named Zebedee who had two sons. Their names were James and John. They had just returned home. They had been traveling with Jesus. They had much to tell about the wondrous words He spoke and of the miracles He performed.

These brothers had two friends who had also traveled with Jesus. They were fishermen. Their names were Andrew and Peter.

The fishermen gathered in groups and listened to the amazing stories which the four friends of Jesus had to tell. When they returned to their homes they repeated the stories to their families.

The women carried the news to the marketplace. The children went to school and told their friends about the wonder of the miracles Jesus performed.

The news spread to the upper part of town, where the rich people lived. A wealthy nobleman listened with great hope when he heard about the Teacher who performed wonderful miracles.

This man was a high officer of the court of King Herod. He lived in a fine house. He and his family had everything that money could buy, but they were not happy. There was much grief in their home, for their only son lay sick in bed with a high fever.

Friends were sorry for the poor nobleman whose only son was so sick. His money did not help him. If his son died, he would lose the greatest treasure of his home.

When the nobleman heard about Jesus, there was a ray of hope for his sick child. Jesus had cured many other people. If

He would come to the nobleman's house, He could cure his son.

The rich man was determined to seek Jesus.

"He is not in our city," explained a friend. "Many say He is coming to Capernaum soon, but we do not know when it will be. Jesus is in Cana now."

"I cannot wait until He comes here," cried the nobleman impatiently. "There is no time to be wasted. My son is too sick. He needs help now. I must find Jesus."

He wasted no time. He was not willing to send a servant on such an important errand. He went himself in search of Jesus.

He found Jesus in Cana.

The nobleman pleaded with Jesus. He said, "My son is sick with a fever. Please come with me to his bedside and make him well."

The nobleman's home was almost twenty miles from the place in Cana where Jesus was staying. He knew He did not have to travel that long distance to cure the sick boy. He wondered if the nobleman would believe this.

Jesus said to him, "You would not believe Me, unless you saw signs and wonders."

The nobleman did not know how to reply. He had never seen Jesus perform a miracle. He had heard about Him. He believed He could cure his son. He thought Jesus would want to travel to his home and see the child in order to heal him.

"Return to your home," said Jesus. "Your son is well. You have no more need to be worried."

The nobleman started to walk toward his home. He was no longer worried, for he believed the words of Jesus. On the way he met his servants. They hurried toward him. The nobleman knew they had good news to tell.

"Your son is living," they cried joyfully. "He is well."

"When did he begin to feel better?" asked the happy father.

"It was in the early afternoon, around one o'clock," they said. "His fever left and he was well."

The nobleman smiled. That was the exact time he had talked to Jesus. It was then that Jesus had said the boy was cured.

The happy father hurried with his servants to his home. He wanted to tell his family about Jesus.

The nobleman entered the house. He called to his wife and son. He told the amazing story of the power of Jesus.

"He did not have to come to our home to heal our son," said the nobleman. "He said I must believe that He could make him well. And I did believe!"

That very day the nobleman's family believed in Jesus. They loved Him. They became His followers.

the miraculous draught of fishes

It was very early in the morning. The sun had not appeared in the eastern sky. Some fishermen were in their boats, working the sails to direct their course.

"We may as well go in!" exclaimed Peter, who was one of the fishermen. "We have been fishing all night and have caught nothing."

"Look at this net," added Andrew, who was with him. "It will be some work to clean it. This was the wrong night to go out. Perhaps another time it will be better."

"Call over to James and John," said Peter. "Tell them we are going in."

Andrew called to the fishermen in a boat nearby.

Soon the two boats were heading toward the shore of the Sea of Galilee.

The fishermen stepped out. They anchored their boats. They began to clean their nets. While they worked in the early morning light, they talked together about Jesus.

"There is Jesus now," cried John after a few moments. "Do you see Him walking over there on the beach?"

"It is the Master," said Andrew. "He is coming toward us!"

"Look at the crowd following Him!" exclaimed Peter. "It is so early in the morning and yet they have come to see Jesus and to hear His teachings."

Jesus walked to the shore where Andrew and Peter were cleaning their net. He saw at a glance that the fishermen had caught no fish, although they had been out all night.

"Take Me out in your boat," He said to Peter. "There are so many people here. If you will cast out a short way from shore, I can speak to them from the boat."

Willingly, Peter and Andrew took their oars and rowed a short distance from shore. Then Jesus sat there and talked from the boat, while the people gathered within easy hearing distance on the shore.

When He had finished talking, the people returned to their homes or to their work. Jesus was alone with His close friends.

He spoke to Peter and said, "Let us go out into the deeper water. Take your net and you will get some fish."

Peter was a fisherman. He knew that it was no use to fish in the daytime. The best fishing was at night. And the place where Jesus wanted to go was not the right place to catch fish. Peter thought he should explain to Jesus that they would be wasting their time.

"Master," he said, "we have fished all night and have taken nothing. But if You say we should, we will go out farther. I will let down the net and try."

Peter and Andrew let down the net in the place where Jesus told them.

The two fishermen could not bring it up alone. The net was

heavy with the weight of many fish.

"Call James and John," cried Peter. "We must have help to bring in this draught of fishes."

The two brothers came in their boat, and together the four fishermen labored to pull up the heavy net. Again and again they threw the net into the water. Each time they drew out a great draught of fishes.

This was a miracle that was greater than any other these friends of Jesus had seen. They had watched Jesus cure people who were sick. Each time they had marveled at His Divine Power. But never had they seen anything like this!

The four fishermen brought their boats back to shore. They emptied their nets and cleaned them. The fish were taken and dried. They were salted and pickled and packed for a caravan that would carry them to the market in Jerusalem.

It was the last time the four fishing partners' worked as fishermen. They left their boats.

The four friends went with Jesus. They were His helpers from that time forth.

a joyful sabbath

It was the Sabbath in Capernaum. Early in the morning, families were getting ready to go to the synagogue for services.

The mother in each home was especially busy, urging her family to be ready on time. Children must be watched to see that their faces were clean. The father was sometimes slow in getting ready. Mother had to help him. There was breakfast to prepare. After family prayer, the morning meal was eaten. The mother and father, with their children, left the house. They locked the door. They walked down the street to the synagogue.

The service began at nine o'clock in the morning and usually lasted until noon.

This Sabbath, the streets of the city were bright with the color of people's dresses. Many families were dressed in their best clothes today.

News had spread that Jesus was going to speak at the service. From all parts of the city the people came to hear Him.

From the upper part of town, where the mansions stood, came the wealthy people. There was the nobleman with his family. Jesus had healed his son when he lay dying of a fever.

There came the ruler of the synagogue. His name was Jairus.

He lived not far from the nobleman.

From another part of town came James and John with their father, Zebedee. Peter and Andrew came, also, to hear the teachings of Jesus.

There were fishermen and farmers at the synagogue. There were merchants. All were dressed in their best clothes.

When they reached the synagogue, the men went to one side and sat down. The women and children occupied another side of the church. The women wore heavy veils that covered their faces.

At one end of the synagogue there was an ark or chest that held the rolls of Scriptures. In front of this were special seats for leaders of the synagogue to sit during the service. At one side, in front, was a platform where the Scriptures were read to the people who gathered in the synagogue.

When it was time for the service to begin, a leader stood before the congregation. He repeated a creed that was familiar to all. Then there were eighteen prayers said in front of the Ark. After each prayer, the congregation said a loud Amen. There was a benediction and then came the most important part of the service. There were seven people who were called upon to read a part of the Scriptures. They reached into the Ark. They drew out a scroll and read that part from the Holy Word which was assigned for the Sabbath.

It was now time for the speaker to talk to the people.

Most of the speakers in the synagogues scolded the people and told them they must do this and that. They seemed to forget to talk about God's great love for them.

Today all eyes were turned toward Jesus, for He was the speaker that Sabbath. The people listened with new interest, for He talked to them about things they knew and understood. Jesus told the people about His Heavenly Father.

While He was talking, a man called out loudly, "What have we to do with You? I know who You are. You are the Holy One of God!"

With pity Jesus sought the man who was calling wildly to Him. This man was sick and needed help. Jesus healed him there in the synagogue, in the middle of the Sabbath service.

When the service was over, the families went to their homes or to the homes of friends for a festive meal. That day Jesus went with Peter to his house.

There was much confusion when they arrived there. Dinner was not ready. Peter's wife hurried to tell her husband that a terrible thing had happened. Peter's mother-in-law had a fever and lay sick on her bed.

Jesus walked into the house. He placed His hand upon the hand of the sick mother. The fever left her and she was entirely well.

That day was one of great rejoicing and festivity. Peter's mother-in-law was able to rise from her bed. She and her daughter prepared the meal and the happy family served Jesus, the Welcome Guest, who was in their home that day.

The sun was setting in the Sabbath sky when the sound of many footsteps was heard outside the home of Peter. Many people were at his door.

These people knew that the Sabbath was a day of rest, but when the sun had set, the Sabbath was over.

They had watched the sun in the western sky until it had lowered and finally disappeared from sight. Then they came in search of Jesus.

There was a mother holding her sick child. A man hobbled on crutches. Another man was led by his friends to the house of Peter because he was blind and could not find his way. All these and many more came that evening to Jesus to be healed. And He helped them.

That day many people believed that Jesus was God's Son, who had come to help them. Their Scriptures had said He would come and bear the sickness of the people and make their burdens His own.

Surely that Sabbath, Jesus took the troubles of God's people away from them. He brought happiness to them when they were sad. It was a joyous Sabbath!

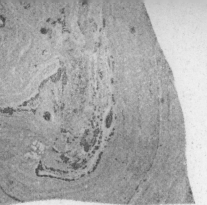

four
helpful friends

Have you ever been a helper? How did you feel when you helped somebody?

You were happy, weren't you? You were happy because you made someone else glad. It is good to be a helper!

The happiest people in the world are those who are always trying to help others. That is why Jesus was happy when He was on earth. He was always helping other people.

Those people who tried to be like Jesus found that they, too, were happiest when they were thinking of others and trying to help them.

There were four friends who wanted to be helpers. They knew a man who was sick. He could not get up from his bed. He could not help himself. His family had to take care of him.

The sick man and his friends had heard that Jesus was in Capernaum. They knew that He had healed many people who were ill. The sick man wanted to go to Jesus. He believed that the Master could make him well. But he did not know how he could be moved from his home.

His friends knew what to do.

"We shall make a bed that we can carry. We shall put you on

71

the bed and take you to Jesus," said one of the friends.

That is exactly what they did. The four friends carefully moved the sick man to a bed which they made for him. They started down the street toward the home of Peter. They had heard Jesus was staying with him.

When the little party turned the corner and arrived at the street where Peter lived, they saw a great crowd of people pushing ahead toward his home. The courtyard by the house was crowded.

"We cannot get very close," said one of the men. "The crowd is too great. I cannot even see the door of the house."

"How will we get to Jesus?" asked the sick man. "I had such high hopes. Now we are so close to Him and yet we cannot reach Him."

"There, there," soothed his friend. "We shall find a way."

The four friends thought of a way to help their friend.

There was a stairway on the outside of the house where Peter lived. It led to the flat roof of his home. This rooftop was often used as a porch, and on hot nights it was a nice place to sleep.

Carefully the four men carried their friend to the rooftop of Peter's home. Then they began using their hands to break open a space in the light roof over the porch where Jesus was teaching.

The friends of the sick man did not have any trouble in breaking through the roof. They had to work for a while until they had a place opened that was large enough for their purpose.

Jesus was standing near the door of Peter's house. He was talking to the many people crowded around Him. He heard a

noise over His head. He looked up and there He saw that a great hole had been made in the roof above His head.

Four men looked down at Him from the hole in the roof. Then they disappeared. A great bundle appeared at the opening in the roof. Slowly it was lowered with ropes to a spot beside the very place where Jesus stood.

Jesus looked. The bundle was the bed that the four friends had made for their sick friend. They had lowered him through the hole in the roof, to the feet of Jesus.

The sick man was rather frightened. He did not know if Jesus would be displeased. He forgot the real reason why he had come. He forgot that he wanted Jesus to make him well. When he looked at Jesus he was ashamed. He remembered all the wrong things he had done in his life. He was sorry. He wanted forgiveness for his mistakes.

Jesus knew the thoughts of the sick man. He quickly eased his fears.

"Your wrongdoings are forgiven," He said.

The sick man was filled with great joy. He almost forgot that he was still a very sick and helpless man.

Jesus did not forget. He spoke again to the sick man.

He said, "Arise, take up your bed, and go on your way to your house."

Suddenly the sick man had feeling in his arms and legs. He was able to move about.

He raised himself from the floor. He stood up. He rolled the bed which his friends had made for him into a neat bundle. He tucked it under his arm. The man was no longer sick and helpless. He was able to walk on his own two legs, without any help. He was a happy man.

The man's friends rejoiced because he had been healed. Jesus was pleased because He had been able to help the sick man.

The happiest people in the world are those who help others. That is why Jesus was happy when He was on earth. He was always helping others.

the chosen helpers

In Capernaum there was a main highway that led to many towns and villages. From this highway there were six other roads that led to more towns and villages.

People came from all directions along these roads to see Jesus. Willingly, He taught those who came to Him.

Jesus knew there were many more people who lived in the villages and towns along the main highway and the six roads. There were other roads and other villages where families lived, too. Jesus had been sent by God to help these people.

He could not travel over all the roads and visit all the towns and villages. There were too many. If He had helpers, they could go in all directions to reach many out-of-the-way places.

Two helpers could take one road and travel along its course. Two other helpers could travel to villages along another road. Twelve helpers could go along six roads and reach out in all directions!

Jesus wanted to choose the best helpers for His work. They were to be His faithful followers. They were to be His close friends.

Jesus wanted to talk to His Heavenly Father about all of these helpers before He called them to Him.

One evening when He was alone He climbed a hillside. It was known as Mount Hattin. In this quiet place He talked to God. All night long He stayed there and prayed.

God let Jesus know the time had come to gather together His helpers.

In the early morning people came to the Mount seeking Jesus. From these followers Jesus chose the twelve men who were to be His special helpers. God, His Heavenly Father, helped Him choose the right men.

Jesus chose the four fishermen who had followed Him for some time. These were His friends Peter and Andrew, James and John. He chose Matthew who had left his job as tax collector to be with Jesus. He chose seven other men.

Jesus was happy. He had twelve helpers who could travel the main highways. They could stop at villages and towns and carry the message of God's love to the families who lived in many parts of the world.

These were the first helpers to spread the story of Jesus throughout the world. From this small group of twelve faithful followers, there have come more and more believers who have learned about Jesus.

Today many, many people know about Jesus because these twelve chosen helpers began to tell about Him, centuries ago, when He lived on this earth.

the sermon
on the mount

Jesus had chosen twelve helpers and He was glad about it.
There was so much He wanted to tell them. They had gathered
at Mount Hattin. This was a quiet place in the hills where He
could talk to them.

There were others who knew that Jesus was on the Mount.
They followed the long road from Capernaum to the quiet place
He had chosen.

Fathers and mothers brought their children up the hillside.
There was a little boy holding tight to his father's hand. There
was a mother carrying her baby daughter. There were fishermen.
There were men who had traveled far. There were teachers who
had come to hear Jesus, the Great Teacher, talk to them.

Jesus looked at the crowd gathered on the Mount. These were
God's children. He loved every one. Jesus talked to them as He
would to one big family.

Each listener to the words of Jesus caught a message that
seemed especially for him.

"Are you wondering where you will get food to eat and
clothes to wear?" asked Jesus.

"Oh, yes," thought a tradesman. "There have not been many customers coming to my shop. I have not earned much money. I cannot buy things that are needed in our family! At night I cannot sleep because I worry—"

"Do not worry," continued Jesus. "God loves you. He is your Heavenly Father. He knows you need food to eat and clothes to wear."

"God does indeed know our needs," said a farmer. "He sends sunshine and rain to make seeds grow in my ground. They bloom and ripen, and they become good vegetables to eat at our table. God has been good to our family."

"If your son asks you for some bread, do you give him a stone?" asked Jesus.

"I would not do such a thing to my child!" exclaimed a father.

"God is your Heavenly Father," said Jesus. "Do you not think He will give you what you need? He loves you. He feeds the birds. He clothes the flowers of the fields in rich colors. Are you not much more important than these to God?"

"It is good to think of God, my Heavenly Father, taking care of me," said a humble fisherman.

"When you know how God loves you," said Jesus, "then your heart will be filled with love for Him. You will love God so much you will want to think of Him at all times. When you put God first in your life and believe in Him, you will know that He will take care of you because of His great love for you.

"Seek ye first the kingdom of God and His righteousness, and all these other things shall be added unto you. You will have clothes to wear. God will give you food to eat. He will provide a safe shelter for you. My God shall provide all your needs, according to His riches in heaven," said Jesus.

"Talk to God as you would talk to your father," said Jesus. "Ask and it will be given to you, seek and you will find.

"I tell you, if two of you on earth agree to ask for anything, My Father in heaven will do it for you, for where two or three have come together in My Name, there I am among them."

The worried tradesman was no longer sad. This message of Jesus gave him new hope.

"How I love God!" exclaimed the tradesman. "With loving care He provides for my family. We have only to ask and He hears our prayers. God's love is so great, He has sent His Son to us. I want to put God first in my life. We must put God first in our family."

jesus
stills the storm

The Sea of Galilee was beautiful in the night light. The waves rippled gently, causing the small boats anchored at the wharf to rock slightly to and fro.

It was the time of night when most people were in their homes.

Jesus stood by the seaside, looking at the rippling waters. It was peaceful and quiet.

Jesus was tired. He had been busy all day. The thought of going into a boat and sailing on the sea seemed a very good idea.

Jesus called to His friends.

"Let us go out to sea," He said.

His friends did not question Him. One of the disciples untied his boat and brought it to a landing place. Jesus and the others entered the boat. Sails were raised. The soft night breeze caught the white sails. They unfurled and opened out into their full size. The boat rocked gently as it rode the light waves of the sea.

The gentle rocking soothed Jesus. He was very tired, so He went to the stern of the boat. Soon He was fast asleep.

The boat sailed until all sight of land was gone. As far as the eye could see, there was water. The small sailing party had reached the middle of the sea.

Suddenly the waves became rough. The sky darkened. A great cloud gathered over the far shore. Heavy rain began to pour down.

There were some experienced sailors in the boat. Peter and Andrew had been fishermen before they became followers of Jesus. James and John had been their partners. These men had weathered many storms on the Sea of Galilee. They knew how to handle a boat in a storm.

The waves gained new strength. The sea rose and fell with such force that the boat was tossed about like a small toy. The waves were so large they almost swamped the boat. The wind blew torrents of rain over the men as they huddled together in fright.

These experienced fishermen had never seen a storm like this. They did not know what to do. They were in the middle of the sea. They could not get to shelter. If the storm continued, the force of the waves might wash them from the boat. The boat could be swamped with water and sink!

All this time, Jesus slept quietly in the back of the boat.

The friends of Jesus became more and more frightened. There was nothing they could do as sailors to save themselves. They must call on Jesus, the landsman, to help them.

The disciples went to Jesus, where He lay sleeping in the back of the boat.

They cried, "Lord, save us or we shall die!"

Jesus awoke. His face was wet with rain. His soaked clothes clung to His body as He rose from the damp resting place. He stood before His beloved disciples, with the winds and rains whipping around Him.

In the face of the terrible storm, when all hope seemed to be gone, Jesus calmly looked out upon the raging sea and spoke.

"Peace! Be still!" He commanded.

The wild winds stopped blowing. The blinding rain stopped falling.

A great calm settled down upon the sea. The waves ceased their rolling. The boat no longer tossed up and down in the water.

The friends of Jesus looked in amazement at their Lord. He had given a quiet command and the terrible storm had ceased. Jesus had power to order the forces of Nature to obey His will. Only the Son of God could perform such a miracle.

Jesus spoke to His friends in the boat.

"Why are you so fearful?" He asked them. "Have you not enough faith?"

The friends lowered their heads in shame. They had called upon Jesus when they needed help. They had been fearful, lest they drown. They needed to trust Him more and more each day.

When Jesus stilled the raging storm, they learned another lesson in trust.

the
WORRIED FATHER

All night long Jairus paced up and down the wharf at Capernaum. He was waiting for Jesus.

He knew that Jesus had gone in the boat with His friends in the early evening. The boat had disappeared from sight. It was far out at sea.

In the night the terrible storm came up. In the storm stood Jairus, looking out to sea, hoping to catch sight of the boat in which Jesus was a passenger.

The wind tore at his garments. The rain drenched his body, but he did not notice it. He was waiting for Jesus!

The minutes went by. The hours dragged on. Still there was no sight of the boat that had carried Jesus out to sea.

Jairus continued to pace the wharf. It was getting late. Perhaps it was too late for Jesus to be of help. But Jairus did not want to think about this. He would not give up. He knew that Jesus could help, if He came in time. Jairus believed this with all his heart.

Jairus was a worried father. His only daughter lay sick in her bed. Each hour she became worse. It did not seem possible that she would live much longer.

Jairus knew that Jesus could help her. He could make her well. But Jesus was gone. He was out at sea in the terrible storm.

Jairus waited all night long, watching for the boat that would bring the Saviour to him.

Finally the mighty storm stopped its awful raging. There was a great calm upon the sea. Daylight came. And still Jairus waited for Jesus.

At last he saw the boat in the distance. He waited eagerly for its arrival at the wharf.

As soon as Jesus stepped from the boat, Jairus rushed to Him. He fell at the feet of Jesus and begged Him to go to his home and cure his sick daughter.

Jesus pitied the worried father. He was glad to help Jairus. He left the seashore and walked up the crooked streets of Capernaum toward the home of the sick child.

It was hard to make any headway. People were jamming the streets. They had heard that Jesus was in the terrible storm. News had reached some of them that a great miracle had taken place in the middle of the sea. Jesus had commanded the storm to be still and a great calm had come upon the waters. The wonder of this had spread about town and many people were talking about it.

Jairus was impatient. Each hour of delay brought his daughter nearer death, for she was becoming weaker and weaker.

The crowd pushed and shoved. Jairus and Jesus tried to make some headway along the streets, but they were unable to hurry their footsteps.

Then Jairus saw one of his servants coming toward him. He feared the news that he brought.

"It is too late," whispered the servant to the father. "Your daughter is dead. Don't trouble the Master anymore."

Jairus bowed his head in deep sorrow. All night long he had waited and watched for Jesus. He had been so hopeful when at last Jesus had returned from the sea and was on His way to their home. But it was all too late. Jairus's only daughter was dead.

Jesus looked upon the grieving father. But He did not feel sad. He had not lost hope.

"Fear not," Jesus said to Jairus. "Only believe. Keep trusting Me."

Jairus looked at the Master in unbelief. How could his daughter be helped when she was dead? It was too late to do anything for her.

They continued their journey through the streets until at last they reached the home of Jairus.

There was much sadness. Friends and relatives were gathered to mourn the death of Jairus's only daughter. Hired mourners were loudly wailing. Flute players were playing mournful tunes.

Jesus gave some commands. He sent away the hired mourners. He told the flute players to leave. He told the relatives to leave.

Jesus spoke to His close friends who had followed Him to Jairus's home. They were Peter, James, and John. These three, together with the mother and father, entered with Jesus into the room where the girl lay dead.

Jesus gently placed His hand on the face of the still child.

He said, "My little girl, rise up."

The child's eyelids fluttered. A healthy pink glow came into her cheeks. Her hands moved.

The young girl opened her eyes. She looked into the kind face of Jesus. She took His hand and slowly rose from her bed.

Jairus's daughter was alive! She was well!

Tears of joy and gratitude ran down the cheeks of Jairus. He had put all his faith in Jesus, and the Saviour had given life to his little girl. It had been a great test of the father's faith. Jesus was glad to see Jairus's faith when all seemed lost.

a
Boy's Lunch

Boys and girls like to eat. They want to be certain that they have something to eat when it is mealtime.

So it was with a young boy who wanted to see Jesus. He heard that Jesus had gone in a boat with His disciples across the sea to a quiet place. This boy did not have a boat to follow the Master, but there was a path around the sea that could be traveled by foot. The young lad decided to follow this road until he came to the place where Jesus and His friends were.

He did not know how long he would be away from home, so the boy took a lunch of two small fish and five loaves of barley bread. When he was hungry he would have food to eat.

This boy was not the only one who wanted to see Jesus. There were thousands of people who heard that the Master had crossed the sea in a boat. They, too, knew about the footpath that led around the shore. They hurried along this road until they came to the place where Jesus was talking to His disciples.

Now, Jesus had wanted to spend some time alone with His helpers. But He knew these people had walked many miles to reach Him. He could not send them away.

He climbed a hillside and stood before the people and talked

to them. Friends and relatives had brought sick ones the long distance around the sea, hoping that Jesus would cure them. Jesus had pity on these people and made them well.

All eyes were on Jesus. All ears were listening to His words. There was no thought of time.

The day was almost over and none of the people seemed ready to leave. They had been there many hours. They needed food to eat, but only the young lad had thought to bring a lunch along.

The disciples of Jesus became worried. The sun was low. Soon, they knew, the sudden darkness would come down upon these people, and they would be without food in this lonely place. It would be some time before they could find their way back along the path to the villages where they could get something to eat.

Jesus knew what He would do about this, but He wanted to test His disciples.

He spoke to Philip and said, "How are we to buy bread so that these people may eat?"

Philip looked at the great crowd that had gathered. There were over five thousand people! He tried to figure in his mind the amount of bread it would take to feed so many people and how much money it would take to buy the bread.

"Two hundred pennyworth would not give each of them enough to eat," replied Philip.

This was a large amount of money. It would have taken one man two hundred days to earn that much!

The disciples urged Jesus to send the people on their way. But Jesus did not listen to His disciples. He told them to see if there

was someone in the crowd who had brought food.

It was Andrew, another disciple of Jesus, who found the boy who had brought his own lunch. He told Jesus about it.

"There is a lad here who has five barley loaves and two fish," said Andrew. "But what are they among so many people?"

One barley loaf was the size of a small bun. The fish were little ones. The boy's lunch was just enough to feed one person.

Jesus said to His helpers, "Make the people sit down."

The disciples were puzzled. They did not know what Jesus was going to do. But they obeyed Him. They divided the people into groups and had them sit on the thick, green grass.

Jesus took the bread and the fish that belonged to the young lad. He stood before the great crowd and said a prayer of thanks.

Then he broke the bread into small pieces and handed them to His disciples. He passed the fish to them.

When the helpers began to pass the food around, there was enough to serve all the people.

When everybody had eaten, Jesus spoke to His disciples and said, "Gather up the pieces so that nothing is lost."

The disciples obeyed their Master. Lo and behold, they brought to Him twelve baskets of food that were left.

Somewhere in that crowd was the young lad who had brought a small lunch for himself. Jesus had taken that little lunch. He had blessed it and given thanks for it. Jesus had performed a wonderful miracle. With five small barley loaves and two fish, He had fed five thousand people!

Jesus Walks on the Water

The twelve disciples of Jesus were not afraid when He was with them. They knew they had the loving, watchful care of their Master. But when they were alone, they were sometimes like frightened sheep without a shepherd. They did not know what to do without Jesus.

One night the disciples were alone in their boat on the Sea of Galilee. They had been with Jesus all day.

Now Jesus had gone up into a mountain, apart from everyone, to pray to His Heavenly Father.

The disciples got into the boat and began to row across the sea.

A terrible storm came sweeping down the barren hills to the sea. Great mountains of foaming, raging water tossed the little boat and threatened to cover it.

The disciples were very frightened. They cried aloud to one another.

"Where is the Master? He promised to meet us. We need Jesus now!"

But even as they called, they had little hope that Jesus could help them, for they knew He was on the mountainside, far from the raging sea.

The disciples of Jesus forgot that their Master was ever watchful over them. They thought only of their great trouble. They forgot to have faith in Jesus.

Using all their strength, the men continued to row their boat, hoping to guide it to a safe landing place. But their strong arms were powerless against the fury of the storm.

It was early morning. For eight hours the disciples had labored, and were still in the middle of the sea. Their own strength had not helped them in this time of need.

Then, in the gray light of dawn, the disciples saw a sight that filled them with terror.

A figure was walking on the sea. It was moving in their direction!

"It is a ghost!" they cried.

But a voice they knew and loved spoke to them, saying, "Be of good cheer. It is I. Be not afraid."

The disciples could hardly believe their ears. Jesus was speaking to them!

They looked again at the figure that was coming toward them. They could scarcely believe their eyes. Jesus, their beloved Master, was walking on the waves of the sea!

Peter wanted to be certain that the figure was Jesus.

He cried out, "Lord, if it is You, let me come to You on the water."

"Come!" said Jesus.

Peter looked into the face of Jesus. He knew his beloved Master was near. All his fear was gone. Peter wanted to be close to Jesus. He wanted to touch His hand.

Peter stepped over the side of the boat. Looking toward Jesus, he began to walk on the water.

He had gone only a little way when he looked down. He saw the churning water at his feet.

"What am I doing?" thought Peter. "I can't walk on water! I am afraid!"

In that moment Peter began to sink into the waves.

"Lord, save me!" he cried.

Jesus put forth His hand. He caught the struggling disciple and helped him into the boat.

When they were safely in the boat, the wind ceased and the storm passed. There was a great calm.

"Oh, man of little faith," said Jesus, "why did you doubt?"

The other disciples knew that Jesus was speaking to Peter. But to each one of them came the same question. Why did he himself have such little faith? Why had he been afraid? Why had he doubted?

The twelve disciples knelt before Jesus in the boat. Humbly they worshiped Him.

Jesus had calmed the raging sea. He had walked on the water to their boat, to save His disciples.

"Truly, You are the Son of God!" exclaimed His disciples.

the transfiguration

It was night.

Peter, James, and John lay stretched out on the grass. They had removed their cloaks and used them as a covering against the cool night air. They had said their nightly devotions. They were ready for sleep.

The three friends looked about them. It was good to be in this quiet place. They felt safe and secure from all harm, for near them was Jesus, their beloved Friend. His head was bowed in prayer. He was talking to His Heavenly Father.

The men were tired, for they had walked many miles that day with Jesus. He had brought them to a place far away from the Sea of Galilee. They had climbed the side of a mountain called Hermon. When darkness came, Jesus had chosen a sheltered spot where His friends could rest for the night while He prayed to God.

It was a beautiful night. The disciples breathed the clear, pure mountain air. They looked about them once more before they closed their eyes in sleep.

In the distance they could see the snow-covered peak of the mountain. In the pale moonlight it glistened like a beautiful

100

sparkling crown. The stars were twinkling in the sky.

The friends of Jesus closed their eyes. They did not know that when they opened them again they would see the most beautiful sight they had ever beheld. This was a night to be remembered!

Peter, James, and John rested for a while. They did not know how long it was. Suddenly they opened their eyes.

They saw a strange light!

It was not the light of a new day. It was not the moonlight shining on the glittering snow of the mountaintop.

It was a dazzling white that was brighter than anything they had ever seen in all their lives!

With wondering eyes, they saw that it was Jesus who was transfigured before them. He had changed from the earthly person that they knew. A heavenly light shone within Him. His garments were glistening white. His face shone as bright as the sun!

As the disciples gazed in wonder at the Master, there appeared Moses and Elias from heaven and they began talking to Jesus.

The disciples were suddenly filled with terror. Yet, at the same time, they were overjoyed at the sight of this vision that no other man had seen.

As they watched, a bright cloud came down from heaven. It overshadowed the mountain.

The voice of God came from the cloud saying, "This is My beloved Son, in whom I am well pleased. Hear ye Him!"

The disciples bowed down. They hid their faces from the shining glory of God.

The bright cloud lifted and disappeared. The heavenly figures of Moses and Elias soon vanished.

Jesus stood alone. And the light that had shone within Him was gone.

Jesus touched His kneeling friends and said, "Arise! Do not be afraid."

The three friends stood up. They looked around. They saw no one there but Jesus.

This was a night that was never forgotten in the lives of Peter, James, and John.

Many times Peter had said to Jesus, "You are the Son of God."

Now, God Himself said the words to Peter and James and John.

"This is My beloved Son, in whom I am well pleased. Hear ye Him!"

who
is to Be first?

When little children are playing games, they very often have to decide who shall be the leader.

One will raise his hand and shout, "First!"

Another child will shout, "I'm second!"

Then there are all kinds of shouts of "Third!" "Fourth!" "Fifth!" until each one knows when it is his turn.

The one who is first, or the leader of the game, is quite happy. He is the most important one!

Grown people like to be leaders, too. They like to be first. They don't raise their hands and shout about it, but they are very happy when they are chosen to be in charge of something. They are proud of themselves. They know that other people look up to them.

There were twelve disciples of Jesus. They, too, wondered who among them was first in the love of their Master. They wondered which of them would be the greatest in the kingdom of heaven.

The twelve men began to argue among themselves.

They were returning from upper Galilee to their beloved city of Capernaum. Jesus was ahead of them, walking alone. The

disciples stayed behind Him. In groups of two and three, they walked.

"The Master talks about His kingdom," said one of the disciples. "When He is the king, we should surely be His chosen subjects."

"I think we should, too," said another disciple. "After all, Jesus chose the twelve of us to be His special helpers. There were many others who wanted to be His followers, but He did not take them."

"Jesus seems to favor those three," said one man, and he pointed to Peter, James, and John. "Do you suppose they will have the best place in the kingdom of Jesus?"

There was no answer to this question. Each disciple was wondering about himself. Would he be the greatest in the kingdom? Each disciple hoped that Jesus would choose him.

All this time Jesus had walked ahead of His helpers. He heard

them arguing. He could not hear what they were saying, for they were careful to speak in low voices. The disciples did not want their Master to know what they were talking about.

Jesus let them alone. He did not say anything to them while they were traveling to Capernaum. He waited until the next day, when they were all together in Peter's house.

Jesus sat down. The disciples stood around Him, Then He questioned them.

"Why were you arguing yesterday when we were on the road?" He asked.

The disciples were silent. They were ashamed. They hoped the Master had not heard them. They looked at one another. Not one of the men looked at Jesus. Each one waited for the other to answer the question that Jesus asked. And, yet, they did want to know which one of them should be the greatest in the kingdom of heaven.

Jesus knew their thoughts. He had an answer for them.

There was a young child in the house. Jesus called him to come closer. He put His arms around the youngster.

"You see this child?" He asked His disciples. "He loves and trusts Me. He believes what I tell him. When I ask him to do something, he does it. He is meek and humble."

Jesus looked at His disciples.

He said to them, "You have high hopes for yourselves. You know I have chosen you to be with Me. We have been together many months. You have been My helpers. Now you are wondering what reward you shall receive for this. You want to know which shall be the greatest among you. You want to know what exalted position will be yours in the kingdom of heaven."

The disciples hung their heads in shame.

"Each one of you wants to have a high place in the kingdom of heaven. I shall tell you how to have it," said Jesus. "Take this child as your example. Believe in Me. Be meek and humble, as this child. And whichever one of you can be most like this child, he will be the greatest in the kingdom of heaven."

The twelve grown men looked at the young child.

The lesson Jesus had taught them was not an easy one. They had much to learn.

Most of all, they knew they must learn to have faith in Jesus, as this child had. They must not argue among themselves and worry about which of them would be the greatest. They must be unselfish. Each must have enough love in his heart to think of the other disciples before he considered himself.

how many times shall i forgive?

Has anyone ever done something to you which made you very angry? Did you want to get even with him? Or did you forgive him?

Peter had a quick temper. He was easily excited. If someone made him angry, it was easier for Peter to try to get even than it was for him to say, "I forgive you for what you have done to me."

One day Peter asked Jesus about this.

He said, "How often shall I forgive someone who wrongs me? As many as seven times?"

Peter thought he was being very kind when he offered to forgive someone as many as seven times. The teachers of the synagogues said a man should forgive another man three times for a wrongdoing, but after that he did not have to forgive him.

Peter had added many more times to that.

Jesus had a different answer than the one Peter expected.

Jesus said, "I do not say seven times, but seventy times seven!"

Peter figured this out in his head. Seventy times seven was four hundred and ninety! Jesus meant that he should always

forgive a person who had harmed him. This was not an easy thing to do.

Jesus told a story to Peter in order to explain what He meant. This was the story.

There was an Oriental king who had many men working for him. They handled the money of his kingdom. At a certain time of the year the accounts were settled.

There was one worker who could not account for a very large amount of money. He had taken more than ten thousand talents, or gold coins, from the king's funds.

The king was very angry. He called the worker to him.

"You have taken my money," cried the king. "You must be punished! You and your wife and children must be sold as slaves. All your possessions shall be sold."

The worker fell at the feet of the king.

"Please have pity on me," he begged. "Give me time. I will pay you everything that I owe."

The king knew that his workman could never repay all the money he had taken. But he had pity on him.

He said, "I will let you go. You and your family are free! As for the money, you could never repay such a large amount, so I will cancel the debt. You are forgiven for what you have done to me."

The workman left the king. He was happy to be free. The king had been good to him.

This same workman had a servant who owed him a small amount of money, only a hundred pence. He was very angry because his servant had not paid.

The workman went to the servant. He seized him by the throat and shook him.

"Pay me the money that you owe!" he commanded.

The poor servant fell to his knees and begged for mercy.

He said, "Please be patient. Give me time. I will repay all that I owe you!"

The workman refused his servant. He threw him in prison. He said he must stay there until the money was paid to him.

There were some other servants who worked in the household. When they heard about their fellow servant, they were sad. They wanted to help him.

They went to the king and told him what had happened.

When the king heard the story, he was very angry with his workman. He called him to come to him at once.

Said the king, "You wicked man! You owed more money than you could ever return to me. But I forgave you. When you found your servant owed you a very small amount, what did you do? Did you forgive him? No! You threw him in prison! Shouldn't you have had mercy on your servant, as I had mercy on you?"

The workman knew he had done wrong. He deserved whatever punishment the king decided upon.

The king was angry. He gave a command. He ordered the workman put in prison.

That was the story Jesus told to Peter when Peter asked the question, "How many times should a man forgive another for doing something wrong?"

Jesus said, "How many times have you done things that were not pleasing to God? How many times has God forgiven you?"

"God forgives me every time I ask Him," said Peter.

"Then you know the answer to your own question," said Jesus. "If God forgives you every time you ask Him, you know how you should treat someone who hurts you. You should not want to get even with him. You should forgive him as your Heavenly Father forgives you!"

the
mustard seed

Many months had passed since Jesus sent His twelve disciples to tell others about the love of God.

There were many places to be visited. In all directions there were towns and villages where families lived who did not know about Jesus.

More messengers were needed to tell how God had sent His Son into the world to give everlasting peace and joy to all who believed in Him. So Jesus chose seventy more disciples to be His helpers.

Some people wondered why He chose that number.

There were others who nodded their heads wisely and said, "Are there not seventy nations in our world today? Jesus has chosen that number for a purpose. He wants us to know that all the people in the world, not just his neighbors, should know about Him.

"Jesus was not sent to this earth to help only a few. God sent His Son to everybody in the world who will love Him and believe in Him."

When the seventy disciples were ready, Jesus divided them in twos. He sent them out in all directions to tell the message of God's wonderful love to all people.

When the disciples returned, they were happy to tell Jesus about their journeys and how they had been received in the homes of those who lived along the roads.

Jesus listened to their stories, and He was glad for the good work they had done.

Then He thought about the great wide world and the millions of people living in it. His twelve disciples and the other seventy messengers could never reach everyone, everywhere, to spread the story of God's love.

Jesus knew His helpers were happy about their missionary journeys. But He also knew they would become discouraged when they thought of the many people who had not been reached. So He told His followers about the mustard seed.

In those days, if a man wanted to talk about something that was very small, he would say, "It is as tiny as a mustard seed."

"A mustard seed is the least of all the seeds that are sown in the earth," said Jesus.

His listeners nodded their heads in agreement.

Jesus then told a story about a man who had a garden. He

planted many seeds there. They were all sizes. Their colors were different and even the shapes of the seeds were not the same. One of the seeds was a tiny yellow one. It was no larger than a pinhead.

The gardener held it in the palm of his hand. The seed was so tiny that it seemed impossible for it to grow in the ground and reach any size that could be noticed.

The gardener knew about the mustard seed. He knew that it grew faster and became greater than all the other plants in his garden.

He took the seed and planted it in the ground. And he waited for it to grow.

In a few days there were two little green leaves pushing through the earth. In a short time the plant grew and grew until it was taller than all the other plants around it. It had many branches and it looked like a tree. The branches were so strong that the birds came and made their nests in them.

"The mustard seed is the least of all seeds, yet see how quickly it grows," said Jesus. "It spreads and spreads so even the birds can find shelter in its branches.

"The kingdom of God is like the mustard seed."

The followers of Jesus knew what He meant. They were few in number when they thought of the great wide world with all the people living in it. They were as small as the mustard seed. Yet, when they told the story of Jesus, it would spread and grow quickly. It would grow greater, until many people, in countries all over the world, would find shelter and comfort in the story of Jesus and God's wonderful love.

the ten Lepers

There are two little words that are easy to say, but some boys and girls, and even grown folks, have a hard time saying them. The words are simple, and they do much good when they are used.

Can you guess what they are?

The words are, "Thank you!"

There were ten men who should have said thanks to Jesus because He did so much for them. How many do you suppose remembered to say it?

These ten men were lepers. That means they had a very dreadful sickness which kept them away from everybody. They had to leave their families and dear ones. They had to live away from the village.

Lepers could not go near anybody who was well.

If a person came close to them, the lepers had to cry, "Unclean! Unclean!"

Now, the ten sick men lived outside a village in Samaria. They had no hope of being well. They could never return to their homes and their loved ones. They had to beg for whatever food they could find. Their clothes were torn and ragged.

Then, one day, they saw Jesus walking toward them. He was on the road that led to their village. These men had heard about Jesus. He had cured many other people. Could He cure a hopeless sickness like theirs? Could He make their skins clean and pure?

The lepers dared not go one step nearer the road. But there was something they could do! They could call to Jesus to help them. When He heard their cries, He might feel sorry for them.

The men stood where they were and cried loudly, "Jesus! Master, have mercy on us! Have mercy on us!"

Jesus heard their cries. He was sorry for the ten lepers.

He called an order to the men.

"Go show yourselves to the priests!" said Jesus.

He spoke to them as if they were already cured. It was a law that a leper could never go near other people unless the priests

119

of the Temple said he was truly well.

These lepers were not cured at the very moment Jesus called to them. But there was power in the words He said which made the ten men start on their way to the priests, as they had been told. As they walked along, they could feel a change coming about. They could see their skins becoming pure and clean from all spots. They were well! As soon as the priests pronounced them cured, they could go home to their loved ones. They could live like other people. No longer would these men have to be outcasts from the village!

Nine men hurried on their way.

One man stopped in the road. He could not go on until he had said thanks to the One who had brought this great happiness to him. He praised God at the top of his voice. Instead of crying the dreaded words, "Unclean! Unclean!" he cried out his thanks.

When he reached Jesus, he fell at His feet and thanked Him.

Jesus looked down upon this one grateful person who knelt before Him.

He said, "Were there not ten who were cured? Are you the only one to come back and give thanks to God?"

Where were the other nine men?

They were hurrying away. They had no thought of the One who had helped them. They did not have time to say thanks.

Jesus said to the one man who bowed before Him, "Arise and go your way."

He was glad that one had remembered to thank Him.

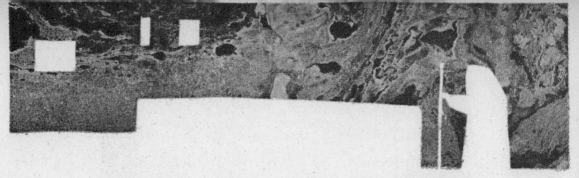

the man who could not see

There was once a man who could not see. He was blind. In all his life there had never been anything but darkness for him.

When he was a tiny baby he could not look into the kind face of his mother. As a small child, he could not search for her when he was suddenly afraid. As a growing boy, he soon learned he could not play like the other children. They could skip and hop and run in their games, while he stood by, listening to their fun.

When the blind man was grown, he knew that he must earn a living. His parents were poor. They needed his help. But what work was there for a blind man?

There was only one thing he could do in those days. He had to be a beggar.

Each morning he left his home. He felt his way along the streets. He used his hands and his feet to guide himself through the town until he came to a suitable place to beg. There he sat and waited for the sound of footsteps. When he knew someone was passing, he put out his hand for money.

The days were all very much the same to this poor man. There was nothing that happened to make any one day different from the others. There was always darkness for him. Always, he could do nothing but sit and wait and beg.

One day his ears caught the sound of many footsteps. A number of people were coming toward him.

He listened. The people were talking about him! They were asking why this man was blind.

The beggar listened for the answer. He heard a beautiful voice. The One who spoke was Jesus. His friends called Him by that name.

The blind man did not understand all that Jesus said, but there was one sentence that he heard clearly.

Jesus said, "I am the Light of the world."

Alas, for the beggar there was no light. For him there was only darkness.

Then he felt tender hands placing something over his unseeing eyes. It felt like wet earth. He wondered why this was being done to him.

Jesus spoke a soft command, saying, "Go, wash in the Pool of Siloam."

The blind man obeyed.

He stood up and walked in the direction of the pool. He had learned to feel his way to most places near his home. He knew how to reach the Pool of Siloam.

When he arrived, he felt his way to the very edge of the water. He stooped low and cupped his hands. He dipped them into the pool and washed the wet earth from his eyes.

The beggar blinked. Something strange and unbelievable was happening to him. Where there had always been darkness, there was now a gray light. The light became brighter. And brighter

For the first time in his life, he could see!

It is hard to say what the beggar looked at first—the bright sky or the shining sun! A whole new world was before him.

This man had listened to sounds and had touched things about him, but never before had he seen God's beautiful world!

The beggar hurried along as best he could, looking at everything. He had known his way about town by touch and sound. Now as he saw them for the first time, the streets with their houses and shops were strange to him.

He looked into the faces of people he passed on the street. He did not know who they were.

The people stopped and stared at the beggar. He looked like the blind man they knew. But this man could see!

"Isn't this the man who sat and begged?" asked the people.

The beggar cried out, "I am that man!"

Joyfully, he told everybody he met that he was the blind man they had known, but that he had been cured. He could see!

"It was Jesus who helped me," cried the blind man. "He rubbed wet earth on my eyes. He said to go and wash in the Pool of Siloam. I did. And now I am able to see! I tell you, nobody but a prophet of God could have done this!"

The happy beggar proclaimed the news all about the town. Everyone heard of Jesus, who had given sight to a blind man.

The news reached Jesus, and He went in search of the man.

When Jesus approached, the happy beggar did not know Him. He had heard the beloved voice of the One who had made him see. He had felt the touch of those precious, healing hands. But with his seeing eyes, he had not yet looked into the face of the One whom he had been praising.

When Jesus said that He was the Son of God, the beggar rejoiced because he had found Him. He fell at the feet of Jesus. He gave thanks to Jesus and worshiped Him.

The happy man wanted to do more than this.

He showed his thanks by telling others about Jesus, the Son of God. Everywhere he went, he praised the Lord.

Jesus, the Light of the world, had brought light to him, when there had been only darkness.

the
LORD'S PRAYER

Jesus often talked to His Heavenly Father in prayer. When He had something to do, He asked God to lead Him in the right way. Jesus always looked to God for guidance.

One day the disciples watched while Jesus prayed. When He was finished, they asked Him to help them.

They said, "Lord, teach us to pray."

"Here is a prayer you can say," said Jesus. And He told His friends the very prayer that you have perhaps said many times.

The disciples learned the words of the prayer Jesus taught them. They learned something else. They learned how to talk to God.

Today we can say the Lord's Prayer which Jesus told His disciples, and we, too, can learn how to talk to God.

Here is the Lord's Prayer.

Our Father who art in heaven, Hallowed be thy name.

God is to be praised and thanked for His everlasting goodness.

Thy kingdom come. Thy will be done in earth, as it is in heaven.

God always knows what is best for each of His loved ones. We

are to ask for God's help, but we must let Him decide what to do for us. He will lead us in the right path.

Give us this day our daily bread.

God always cares for His loved ones. We are to look to God to provide for all our needs.

And forgive us our debts, as we forgive our debtors.

Let us ask God to forgive all the wrongs we have done. When we ask this, we must remember to forgive any wrong that somebody has done to us.

And lead us not into temptation—

When we ask God to lead us, we know that we will not be tempted to do wrong.

But deliver us from evil.

God will keep us from all harm and danger.

For thine is the kingdom, and the power, and the glory forever. Amen.

Finally, because we know we can always look to God, with His loving care to lead us in the way that is best for us, we want to glorify Him forever and ever.

the
Lost sheep

Sometimes when Jesus was walking through the country He saw many sheep grazing. There was always a man watching over them so they did not stray away and get lost. That man was called a shepherd.

Jesus thought of a story about a shepherd and his sheep.

This shepherd loved his sheep, and his sheep loved him. They knew his voice. They knew their shepherd took good care of them.

Every morning the shepherd went to the fold where the sheep stayed at night. He opened the door and called to them. They rushed to the gate, crowding and jamming together to be the first out of the fold. They wanted to scamper down the road toward the grassy slopes where they could eat all day. If someone besides their own shepherd called to them, those sheep did not leave their fold! They waited for their leader's voice.

Down the road the sheep ran. Some of the younger ones ran to the side, but the shepherd was careful to see that they did not stray from the flock. He carried with him a long staff, or stick. If a little lamb tried to get away, he gently prodded him with his staff and guided him back with the others.

When they reached the pastureland, the shepherd let his sheep roam around where they could find plenty of grass to eat. He was always near, watching each one to see that none strayed from his sight. He knew that if any one of the flock wandered away, a wolf, or even a bear or lion, might be watching quietly. He would spring toward the helpless animal and kill him.

All day long the shepherd watched his sheep. Sometimes he led them to springs of water where they could drink.

When it was noontime, he looked for a shady place to rest. He opened his lunch bag and ate his meal.

Just before dark he started home. The shepherd called to his sheep. He went here and there, and with his long staff he gently guided them along the way.

After a while they reached the gate of the fold. The shepherd hurried ahead. He wanted to count the sheep as they entered the fold to see that not one was lost.

He counted them as they passed him, one by one.

"One sheep, two sheep, three sheep, four, five . . . ninety-six, ninety-seven, ninety-eight, ninety-nine." But what about this? There had been a hundred sheep in the flock. Now there were only ninety-nine.

One was lost!

"What has happened to my little lamb?" said the shepherd to himself. "I must find him!"

He closed the door of the fold. Ninety-nine sheep in his flock were safe inside for the night.

The shepherd started out in search of the one little lost lamb.

He was very tired. He had been busy all day, guiding the

flock, keeping them together as they walked all over the slopes. Now it was dark. He could hardly see where he was going. He stumbled over loose rocks. But the shepherd did not give up and go home to rest. He looked behind bushes and in rocky places. Always he walked and searched and called to the sheep, loud and clear.

"Here, little lamb! Here, little lamb!"

After a long time he heard a soft cry. It was the lost sheep! The shepherd hurried toward the sound. And there was his little lamb!

Gently he lifted the animal and placed him on his shoulders. The lamb was very glad to see the shepherd. He put his nose down and cuddled close to him.

Every step of the way back to the fold the shepherd carried the little lost sheep, although he was very tired from the busy day and the long search through the night. In his heart was great happiness, for he had found his lost one.

When he reached the fold, the shepherd looked carefully at the sheep for any wounds or scratches. Very tenderly he cared for his little lamb. When he was safely bedded in the fold for the night, the shepherd took his place just outside and there he rested for the night, happy that every one of his sheep was now safe!

Jesus was thinking of God when He told this story. God is the Good Shepherd. We are His sheep. He watches over and cares for every one of us. He keeps us safe. If any one of us forgets about God and strays away from Him, He is sad until we return to His protecting care.

who is
my neighbor?

Who is your neighbor? Is he a friend who lives next door? Is he someone who meets you on the street? Is he a stranger who is traveling on the road? Is the boy or the girl who lives in dark Africa, or faraway France, your neighbor? And is the little Japanese child who lives across the ocean your neighbor?

A certain man wanted to know the answer to that very question. So he asked Jesus about it.

He said, "The Bible tells me to love God and to love my neighbor. But who is my neighbor?"

Jesus told the man a story and let him answer the question.

There was a road that led from Jericho to Jerusalem. It was a very dangerous road because there were many robbers who hid among the rocks along the way. They waited until someone came along for them to rob.

One day these wicked bandits saw a traveler walking down the road. They ran from their hiding place. They seized the poor man. They took his moneybag. They searched for all his valuable belongings. They beat him and tore the clothes from his back. Then they ran back to their hiding place, where they divided their loot. They left the poor traveler lying at the side of the road, near to death.

This was a lonely road. Few people came that way. There did not seem to be much hope that help would come for the helpless traveler.

Later on, there were soft footsteps along the rocky path. Around the bend came a man dressed in the clothes of a priest. He had just returned from Jerusalem where he had been performing his duties at the Temple.

He stopped in his tracks. He looked down at the poor, bleeding man.

"I cannot help this man," thought the priest. "I have just been to the Temple. I have on my best clothes. They would become unclean. This man is a traveler. He may not belong to my people."

So he walked away.

By and by a second man came along the lonely road. He saw the wounded man. He walked over to the place where he lay, but he was afraid to stop. If robbers had once come to this place, they might come again. They might seize him and beat him! Anyway, he had to hurry.

So he walked away.

The poor man lay helpless and dying. Two travelers had seen him. They had walked away. Was no one willing to do something for him?

Clickety-clack, clickety-clack! Someone else was coming down the road. Those were the sounds of a donkey walking on the rocky path. A man was riding on the little animal. He was called a Samaritan, because he came from the land of Samaria.

When he came to the place where the poor traveler lay, he

stopped. He alighted from his donkey. He bent over the dying man to see if there was something he could do.

The good Samaritan was not like the other two who had passed that way. He did not worry whether the dying man was from his own country, or from some other place. Whoever he was, the poor traveler needed help. He was a neighbor in distress.

The Samaritan was in a hurry. He had business in another

town. He knew it was dangerous to stop in this place where robbers were hiding, but he had found a man who needed his help. That was more important to him than anything else.

The Samaritan took some supplies from his pack. He knelt beside the dying man. He washed his bleeding wounds and bandaged them. He lifted the traveler very carefully onto the donkey's back.

Down the road they went, the wounded man on the donkey and the good Samaritan walking beside, leading the way.

At last they came to an inn where travelers could stay. The Samaritan lifted the wounded man carefully from the animal. He placed him on a bed. He watched over him all night.

The next day the Samaritan had to be on his way. But he did not leave until he had made arrangements for the stranger he had found on the road.

He went to the innkeeper and said, "Take good care of this man. Here is some money to pay for his lodging and food. If it is not enough, I will repay you when I come this way again."

The good Samaritan went on his way, but only after he had done what was right for the helpless, wounded traveler.

There were three men who passed the dying man who had been attacked by the robbers.

Which of the three was a good neighbor?

The good Samaritan was the good neighbor!

This story answered the question which the man asked Jesus: "Who is my neighbor?"

A neighbor is anyone in all the world who needs help.

Jesus said, "Love thy neighbor as thyself!"

a
BRAVE DISCIPLE

It was wintertime in the Holy Land. The weather was rainy and unpleasant, but that did not keep the people from traveling along the roads from their home villages to Jerusalem for the celebration of the Dedication Festival.

The Temple was crowded with people attending the services. On the porch there were many more people who had come to seek shelter from the rain. They were waiting their turn to go to services in the Temple.

Jesus had come to the Dedication Festival. He stood in the shelter of the porch, watching the worshipers come and go.

Among these people there were many who knew and loved Jesus. They were His faithful followers.

There were some, however, who did not want to believe that He was the Son of God.

Some of these unbelievers who saw Jesus standing on the porch of the Temple stopped to question Him.

They asked, "Are You the Messiah?"

Jesus knew why they asked this question. They wanted to trick Him. If He said He was the Promised Messiah, they could declare that He wanted to overthrow the leaders of the Holy Land and establish His own kingdom on earth.

This was not the plan of Jesus. God had sent Him to help the people. He had not come into the world to overthrow any political leaders.

Jesus answered the questioning crowd of people. He hoped they would try to understand Him.

He said, "The miracles I have performed in My Father's name

and the words I have said have proved that I have been sent by My Heavenly Father to help you."

The listeners did not want to understand what Jesus said to them. They muttered angrily to themselves. Some of the people looked around for stones that they could throw at Jesus. They did not know what they were doing.

Jesus was not afraid when He stood before these unbelievers, but He saw that there was no use talking to them. They would not listen, so He slipped away.

Jesus knew He had many followers. He also knew that in Jerusalem there were those who did not believe in Him and who wanted to harm Him. So He left the city. He took His disciples with Him. He traveled far north to the place where His good friend John the Baptist had preached about Him in the past.

Here the people welcomed Jesus. They had heard many stories from John about the Promised Saviour of the world. They were glad to see Him.

Jesus performed miracles in this land and the people marveled at the power which God had given Him.

The disciples of Jesus listened to the welcome words of the crowd. They were happy to be in this place. They knew Jesus was safe here, away from the angry mob in Jerusalem. They knew they also were safe. They were well known as the followers of Jesus.

It was not possible to stay in this safe shelter very long.

A messenger came one day with news that told of great sorrow in a home that Jesus loved very much.

Mary and Martha sent word from Bethany to Jesus, saying,

"Lord, he whom Thou lovest, our brother Lazarus, is sick."

Jesus was always ready to help His friends when they were in trouble. Most certainly, Mary and Martha needed Him at this time, but Jesus knew what was best to do for them.

He sent the messenger back to Bethany alone. He stayed for two more days in the place where He was. Then He surprised His disciples when He told them of His plan.

"We must go to Bethany," He said.

"How can You return to that part of the land?" they asked. "It is only a short time ago that some of the people near there were trying to harm You. There are enemies in that territory!"

"It is time for Me to go," said Jesus. "I must do the work of God, My Father. Our friend Lazarus has fallen asleep. I must waken him from this sleep."

"Sleep is good for one who is sick," said one of the disciples.

"Lazarus is dead!" said Jesus.

The disciples did not know what to think about this. They wondered why they should return to enemy land when their friend Lazarus was already dead and beyond help.

They could not help but worry about their own safety, too.

Then Thomas, one of the disciples, forgot about himself. He was stouthearted and brave. His love for Jesus made him forget his own danger and think only of his Saviour.

"Let us all go," said Thomas. "If we must risk our lives to be with Jesus, let us show our love by staying at His side."

The disciples left with Jesus. They went back to the land where they knew trouble was waiting for them. They were willing to risk their lives for the sake of their beloved Saviour.

Lazarus raised from the dead

Mary and Martha sat on the floor weeping. Their brother Lazarus was dead. He had been dead four days. His body was buried in a tomb outside the city.

All this time the sisters had wept for their brother.

Many friends had come to comfort them in their sorrow. They sat in the home of Mary and Martha. They wanted to be helpful.

There was one friend who had not come to the sorrowing home in Bethany. Mary and Martha had sent a messenger in haste to Jesus, telling Him when Lazarus was sick. But He had not come to help.

He had sent a strange message saying, "This sickness is not unto death, but for the glory of God."

The two sisters had been hopeful that Jesus would cure their brother, even though He did not come to Bethany. But Lazarus had died. And Jesus had not even come to comfort His beloved friends.

After four days of weeping and mourning for their brother, Martha received word that Jesus was on His way to their home. She did not wait for Him. She hurried out of the house to meet

Him on the road. Martha was glad to see Jesus, but she was sad to think He had come too late to help her brother.

When they met outside the village she said, "Lord, if You had been here, my brother would not have died. But I know that even now, whatever You ask, God will give it to You."

Jesus answered his dear friend Martha and said, "Your brother shall rise again."

Martha did not understand the promise of Jesus. But she believed in Him. She knew He was the Son of God. All of this she told Him as they stood on the road outside the village, and then she left Him. She hurried home to her sister Mary.

"The Teacher is here!" she exclaimed. "He is asking for you."

When she heard the good news, Mary hurried from the house to find Jesus. Martha followed her. And the friends, who had been staying at the home of the sisters in order to comfort them, rose and followed, also.

When Mary saw Jesus she fell at His feet and cried. The friends who had come with her began to cry, also.

Jesus loved Mary and Martha and Lazarus. They were all dear to Him. When He saw the sisters and their friends in tears, He was sorrowful. Jesus wept for these loved ones.

The friends of the sisters said one to another, "See how He loved Lazarus. If He had only come sooner, He might have saved their brother."

"Lord, if You had only been here, Lazarus would not have died," cried Mary.

"Where is he?" asked Jesus.

Mary led the way to the cave where Lazarus had been laid to

rest. There was a great stone in front of the cave.

"Take the stone away," said Jesus.

Martha did not want this to be done. "It is too late," she said. "Lazarus has been dead four days."

"Didn't I tell you that if you would believe you should see the glory of God?" asked Jesus.

Then they took the stone away from the place where Lazarus was buried.

Jesus lifted His eyes to heaven and said a prayer to God.

Then He called in a loud voice, "Lazarus, come forth!"

The friends of Mary and Martha stood trembling at the door of the cave. The two sisters waited anxiously.

From the opening of the cave came Lazarus, who had been dead and buried for four days! He was bound from head to foot in the grave clothes that were put on him when he died. His face was bound with a napkin.

"Unwrap him and let him go," said Jesus.

And Lazarus, who had been carried to his grave four days before, was able to walk happily to his home with his sisters.

Jesus had promised to show them the glory of God, and through this miracle He kept His word.

Many of the friends who had come with Mary and Martha to mourn for the dead brother returned happily to their homes. They saw their friend Lazarus brought to life. They saw a miracle that day which made them believe in Jesus and rejoice in having Him for their friend.

JESUS BLESSES
the chILDREN

There is a story about Jesus that is especially for boys and girls. It is a story about little children of long ago.

They wore different clothes than boys and girls wear today. Their games were not the same. The land in which they lived was not anything like America. But they laughed and played and enjoyed life in much the same way as the children of today.

These little children lived in the time when Jesus was on earth. Their mothers and fathers had seen Jesus as He walked down the streets. They had watched the crowds following Him. They had heard His kind voice. And they had watched when sick people were brought to Him. They had seen Jesus place His hands upon them and make them well.

The mothers and fathers wanted to take their little children to Jesus. They wanted Him to touch their boys and girls. Surely if they could just be near enough for Jesus to lay His hands on them they would be blessed.

Little children had watched Jesus, too, as He walked through their town. They wanted to be close to Him. They wanted to hear Him tell of His great love for them.

There were always so many people around Jesus that the

small children were unable to get close. Sometimes, in the crowd, a little boy could peek through the long legs of people in front of him and see the hem of the garment Jesus wore. Or a tall man might lift a little child to his shoulders so the child could see Jesus.

Then one day some children were able to be very close to Him. Their mothers brought them to Jesus so that He might touch them and give them His blessing.

Nearby stood some of Jesus' disciples. They did not like to be bothered with little boys and girls. They scolded the mothers who brought their young children to Jesus.

They said, "Our Master is busy with more important things. Can't you see that? Do not bother Him. He has no time for you and your little ones!"

The disciples were wrong. Jesus wanted to have the children brought to Him. He wanted to talk to them and hold them close. He wanted them to know of His great love for them.

Jesus said to His helpers, "Let the children come to Me. Don't forbid them, for of such is the kingdom of heaven."

He took the children in His arms. He placed His hands on them and blessed them.

In this way Jesus showed His love for all children.

mary's
gift to jesus

Jesus was always thinking of helping others. Whenever He saw people in trouble, He was ready to help them.

During the winter months Jesus had been traveling through the land with His disciples. He had not stayed in any certain place for a long time, but wherever He went He helped people who came to Him. He healed the sick. He made the lame to walk. He brought sight to the blind.

There were many times when Jesus was weary. He was always helping others, but sometimes He needed someone to comfort and care for Him.

There were friends in Bethany who were waiting to give Him that loving care. They were anxious to serve Jesus, their beloved Master, who was always serving others.

Jesus looked forward to reaching the little town where His friends waited for Him. He and His disciples had been traveling for quite a while. The last part of the trip had been tiresome, as there was a narrow, steep path to climb upward from Jericho to Bethany. It was good to reach a place, at last, where they could rest with friends.

As soon as these friends saw Jesus, they began to make plans to welcome Him. Each friend wanted to do something special for Him.

Simon was a friend. He said, "I shall give a dinner for Jesus and invite His friends. He will want to see them and talk with them. He will be glad to be with those who are dear to Him."

Martha said, "If Simon gives a dinner, I want to do something. I can help with the meal. I can serve Jesus."

And she went briskly about the house of Simon, helping wherever she could, doing those things that made Jesus comfortable and happy.

Martha served the Lord and was happy to do this for Him.

Mary loved Jesus dearly. She wanted to do something for Him, too.

There was a treasure which Mary owned. She decided to use this treasure to show her love for Jesus.

It was an alabaster vase which held some costly ointment. This perfume came from faraway mountains in North India. It had been carried on the backs of camels for many, many miles before it reached the little town of Bethany. Mary had purchased the vase of precious ointment.

While the guests were eating dinner, Mary entered the room carrying the vase in her hand. She went directly to the place where Jesus was eating His meal. When she reached her beloved Master, she broke the top from the vase which she had guarded

so carefully. She poured the precious perfume upon the head and feet of Jesus.

The air was filled with the sweet smell of the rare perfume. Everyone looked toward Mary.

"How foolish to use that expensive ointment!" cried Judas, who was a disciple of Jesus. "If she had used that money for the poor, she could have done more good."

Jesus scolded Judas for this. He knew that Mary had given her precious gift to show her love.

"Leave her alone," said Jesus. "She has done a good work, for she has come to anoint My body with sweet perfume. The poor you have with you always, but I shall not be with you much longer.

"This deed will always be remembered. Wherever the Gospel shall be preached in the whole world, there shall also be told this story of the woman who showed her love for her Master in her own way."

Jesus' statement was most certainly true, for the story of Mary's gift is told four different times in the Bible.

Jesus did not forget the gift of His beloved friend Mary. Jesus does not forget a gift from any of His beloved children.

Today it is not possible to give something directly to Jesus, as Mary did. But Jesus said when anyone gives to a person who needs help, it is the same as if the gift were given to Him.

It is good to know this, for to help others brings gladness to the one who is helped. It cheers the one who is the giver of help, too, and Jesus is glad for both the giver and the receiver of the gift.

the
triumphal entry

The narrow streets of Jerusalem were jammed with men, women, and children. Those who could not wait on the streets climbed to the rooftops along the way. Everywhere, everywhere, there were people waiting in happy expectancy!

What was the reason for all the excitement? Who was coming to the city?

Jesus was coming!

The news had spread like wildfire. So they waited for Him—men, women, and children. On the bridge, by the city gate, along the narrow streets, on the housetops, people waited for Jesus. While they waited they talked excitedly.

"Who is He?" asked a stranger from North Galilee. "I have heard so much about Jesus. He did not come to our village, but news of Him spread even to our faraway part of the land."

"He is the great Teacher. Some call Him a prophet," a man answered, "but I know He is the Son of God. No one else could perform the great miracles that He has."

"So I've heard," said the man from the faraway village.

" 'Tis true," interrupted a second man who had been listening. "Let me tell you about myself. I was a leper. I had given up all hope for a good life, but Jesus made me well. Look at my skin. It is pure and clean. I can live as other people. I tell you, He is the Messiah!"

"In our town Jesus cured many people," said a man from Galilee, and he told his story.

While the people waited for His coming, they told of the wondrous miracles He had performed. Everywhere, men and women told of friends or relatives or neighbors in their villages whom Jesus had helped.

"I was lame, but now I can walk without crutches," cried one man. "Watch me! I do not even limp. See, my legs are strong and sturdy!"

Another man looked all about him. He saw the budding flowers and the green trees. He saw the blue sky. He looked at the people dressed in bright colors. He looked at the flags and banners gaily waving in the streets.

Quietly he said, "I would have seen none of this if Jesus had not come my way. I was blind and He made my eyes to see!"

Along the narrow streets, on the crowded rooftops, by the city wall, at the entrance gate—in all these places, people told of the good deeds Jesus had done during the years He had been among them.

"Jesus blessed my children," said a mother happily.

"I touched the hem of His garment and I was made well," another woman added.

"We were mourning the death of my only son," exclaimed a widow from Nain. "Jesus brought him back to life!"

So the stories were told by people who had gathered from all

parts of the land. Each story showed the loving care of Jesus. Each was a witness to the great work Jesus had done to help God's children.

Suddenly there was an excited stir.

"He is coming now!" cried the people, and all eyes were turned to the road.

Jesus was coming! He was riding on a colt. There was a great crowd of people leading the procession. The disciples were walking proudly beside their Leader. Another great crowd followed behind.

All were praising Him and saying, "Blessed is He that cometh in the name of the Lord. Blessed be the kingdom of our father David, that cometh in the name of the Lord. Hosanna in the highest!"

As the procession drew near, some of the people placed palm branches and myrtle twigs in the road. Others took the cloaks from their backs and spread them in the pathway of Jesus.

This was the triumphal entry of Jesus into the city of Jerusalem.

He was welcomed as a great king. Many who sang praises to Him were those whom He had helped with loving care.

The stories of the happy people from all parts of the land were proof that Jesus had come to the world to help God's loved ones. This day, they were gathered together to sing songs of praise to their leader, Jesus Christ.

This day they sang, "Blessed is He! Hosanna in the highest!"

the children's hosannas

The Temple in Jerusalem was God's House.

Every year many people traveled long distances to this place to celebrate religious feasts. They came to pray to God. These people came from all parts of the land.

Many times Jesus had come to the great Temple. It was His Father's House. He belonged there.

When Jesus looked about Him, He was sad. He was sad because the Temple had changed. It was no longer God's House. The officers who were in charge and the officials of the city changed the Temple. They made it their house for worship but they did not worship God. They worshiped themselves!

God said, "My House shall be a House of Prayer."

But in the Temple the leaders, who were called Scribes and Pharisees, did not know how to love and worship as God asked.

Jesus said, "Love the Lord thy God with all thy heart, and love thy neighbor as thyself."

But the Scribes and Pharisees loved themselves first. They looked down on their neighbors, without love.

This year, too, the people came again to the city of Jerusalem to worship at God's House. The leaders of this holy place opened the doors and welcomed the throngs that crowded into the Temple.

The Scribes and Pharisees did not welcome the most important One who came to their doors. They did not welcome Jesus, the Son of God. This was because there was no room in their hearts to worship anyone but themselves. They had love only for their own selfish beings.

Jesus was sad when He saw the Scribes and Pharisees who pretended they were righteous. In deep sorrow He wept for these leaders of the people who did not have the love of God in their

hearts. There was no hope for them!

There were many people in Jerusalem who believed in Jesus, the Son of God. They crowded together on the Temple porch to welcome Jesus. They were eager to hear true teachings about God's Word.

The leaders of the Temple could not teach them rightly. So Jesus talked to them.

As Jesus taught the people, a choir of children's voices was heard nearby. They were singing, "Blessed is He! Hosanna to the Son of David. Hosanna in the highest!"

Jesus looked about Him. He saw the Scribes and Pharisees walking here and there, very important at their duties, pretending to be so good. He shook His head hopelessly in their direction.

Jesus looked at the eager crowd which had gathered around Him. These people were anxious to hear the Word of God from His own Son, Jesus. Here were many followers.

Then Jesus looked hopefully at the young children who were singing praises to Him.

Here were followers who were growing up. They would soon be men and women. And the love of God was growing within them. Many of these young children would keep the teachings of Jesus ever before them. They would grow to love God with all their hearts. They would remember to love their neighbors as themselves. They would always believe in Jesus.

It was a song of hope and joy for Jesus, the Son of God, when He heard the choir of lovely young voices singing, "Hosanna in the highest!"

JUDAS

Judas was angry. He was angry at Jesus.

How could anyone be angry with a friend as true as Jesus? Judas was one of the twelve men whom Jesus had chosen to be His close friends and followers. How could this one man hate Jesus, when the other eleven loved Him and were so loyal to Him?

Jesus knew that Judas hated Him. The Master knew the reason for this, but He did not hate Judas in return. Instead, He had loving pity for His one follower who had strayed away from doing that which was right.

One night Judas walked alone, thinking black thoughts and making wicked plans. He had left the other disciples with Jesus. He could not think in the room where there was such love as the disciples and Jesus had for one another. He had to be alone to be able to work out the evil plan for hurting his Master.

"How did I ever become a follower of Jesus?" Judas asked himself. "For three long years I have been His disciple. I have gone everywhere with Him.

"He was always talking about His kingdom. So I was glad to be one of His followers. I could be patient! It was worth waiting three years to be one of the head men in a kingdom. I could see a great future for myself as one of the most important men in all the land.

"Now my hopes are gone, and who can I blame for that but Jesus? The very One I have followed these long years has turned down the chance to be a great leader of our people. Look how they clamored for Him the other day when He entered Jerusalem on the colt! They threw their very cloaks in His pathway. They sang songs of praise to Him. They were ready to go into the city and take it over.

"What did Jesus do? He waved it away and said He wanted none of it. He would rather establish a kingdom in heaven! I have waited three years to become a great person, ruling with Jesus and the other disciples, and now there is no hope for that!

"Jesus has ruined my plans. But I can ruin His plans. I can be a traitor. I can turn Jesus over to the leaders of the Temple. They will be glad if I come to them. They know I am one of His chosen followers. I can do great harm to Jesus!"

So the evil Judas trudged in the dark night along the road to

the city gate. The sentries were on guard when he reached Jerusalem. They were not willing to let a stranger enter into the city at a late hour unless he had a good reason.

"I have a message for the high priests and Scribes," said Judas to the guards. "It is about Jesus."

The guards considered for a while, then decided to let Judas

164

into the city. They sent a guard of men with him along the dark streets to the leaders who were also plotting to do some harm to Jesus. These men wanted to hurt Jesus because they were afraid of Him.

Judas was taken before the leaders.

"I am one of the twelve disciples of Jesus," he said.

In the glow of the dull night lamps Judas could see the wily smiles of the men before whom he stood. He knew what they were thinking.

"So, one of His own followers has come to us for a good reason," said a man.

"Yes," replied Judas, "I am willing to turn Jesus over to you if we can reach an agreement."

That night the wicked plotters put their heads together and made plans to take Jesus and to do great harm to Him.

It was a black night. The hate in the hearts of these wicked men made them plan the worst deed that has ever been done in all the history of the world.

The bargain was made. The leaders of the temple gave Judas thirty pieces of silver. In exchange, he arranged a meeting place where their guards could find Jesus and seize Him.

Jesus knew what Judas had done. Jesus did not hate him for this. His love was so great that He had only pity for the one of His twelve who had strayed away and would nevermore find joy or peace for himself.

Judas wanted a high place in the kingdom of Jesus. He would never be there, for Jesus' kingdom was built on love and faithfulness. Judas had only hatred in his heart.

thirteen
pairs of sandals

Outside the door of an upper guest room were thirteen pairs of sandals standing in a row.

It was night, but the light from the moon shone down on the floor where the sandals were placed in pairs against the wall. A twinkling light from the wall lantern cast a yellow glow over the quiet place.

Inside the room sat thirteen men. One of them was Jesus. He was celebrating the Passover Feast with His twelve disciples.

He looked at His beloved friends who were gathered around Him. They were dear to Him. He knew that He was soon going to leave them. There was much He wanted to tell them so that they would be ready for the separation that was coming.

It was almost time to begin the Passover Supper. The disciples had taken their places around the table.

At a feast where there was a servant present, it was his task to take a basin of water and a towel and go from one guest to another, washing their feet.

At this Passover Feast there was no servant, and none of the disciples wanted to take the part of a servant. They had all taken their places at the table and were waiting for someone else to do the task.

Jesus knew He must teach His disciples another lesson in love. They must not be proud. They must not seek the highest places for themselves.

Jesus took a basin of water and a towel. He went from one to the other of His disciples. He began washing their feet. As He went about this lowly task, He talked to them.

"You call Me Master and Teacher. And you are right," said Jesus. "But even though I am your Master, I have washed your feet. I have served you willingly. If I help you, then you must help others. You will be happy doing this. For when you help others, it is the same as if you were helping Me and My Father in heaven.

"He that is greatest among you," continued Jesus, "let him be humble. He that is chief should serve the others. Do you not remember that I am God's Son? Yet I have not required people to wait on Me. I have come to serve others. I give you a new command: Love one another, even as I have loved you."

Jesus washed the feet of His disciples that night in the quiet upper room to show them how to be humble. He, who should have been served, was serving them.

"He that believes in Me, the works that I do, shall he do also; and greater works than these shall he do; because I go to My Father," said Jesus.

The disciples did not know what was ahead of them. Jesus was preparing them for the work they were soon to do for Him when He had gone to His heavenly home.

Jesus had washed the feet of His twelve disciples.

Later, His followers would go outside the door. They would put on their sandals and go on their way.

One pair of feet would lead to trouble and betrayal. Judas's feet would take him to an unhappy ending.

The other eleven pairs of feet would travel to all parts of the land. They would be doing the work of Jesus who had sent them on their way.

Such was the story of the thirteen pairs of sandals. Eleven followed in the right paths of Jesus. One followed the path of evil and destruction.

the
LORD'S SUPPER

All over the city of Jerusalem there were families and friends who had gathered to celebrate the Passover Feast. In each house the celebration was much the same. There was a roasted lamb. There was unleavened bread. There were side dishes and bitter herbs.

At the beginning of the Feast the head of the house took a goblet of wine and held it before him while he said a prayer of thanks. He passed the goblet around for all to sip from it.

The roasted lamb was placed on the long table, with the un-leavened bread and other food. And the Feast was begun.

During the Feast the head of the family told the meaning of the Passover celebration and everyone listened. He told of the time, many years before, when the Israelites had been delivered from being servants in Egypt. Forever after, they had celebrated this great occasion. The blood of the lamb of the Feast was given to the Temple as a sacrifice. And the roasted lamb was a part of the meal in the home where the celebration was held.

Now, in the quiet upper room where Jesus sat with His twelve disciples the Feast was different from those in other homes. Jesus did not tell the Passover story as His friends expected Him to do.

The disciples watched Jesus at the head of their table. He took some bread. Holding it before Him, He blessed it and began to break it in pieces.

He passed the broken bread to each of His disciples and said, "Take and eat, for this is My body which is broken for you."

The disciples did not understand what Jesus was talking about. They realized that He foresaw something that was to happen, but they did not know what it was.

Jesus knew that He was soon to be taken a prisoner. His body would be broken for God's beloved people in all the world.

Then Jesus lifted a wine cup in His hand. He blessed the wine and passed it to each of His disciples.

Again He foretold His death when He said, "This wine is My blood which is shed for the forgiveness of sins."

His blood was soon to be shed as a sacrifice for those who loved Him.

Jesus did not want this solemn occasion to be forgotten.

He said, "As often as you eat this bread and drink this wine, remember Me."

The Feast was ended.

The disciples pondered the words of their Saviour. He had not told them the story of the Passover Feast, as they knew it. He had told them that He was to die for them. He was to be the Lamb that was slain. His blood was to be shed to save them.

It was a sad thought. The disciples grieved for their Master. They wondered what was going to happen to them.

Then Jesus said a beautiful prayer that eased the fears of the worried disciples.

When He talked to His Heavenly Father, these are some of the words He said: "I have finished the work which You gave Me to do. I have told the people the words You gave Me. They have received them. They know and believe in Me as the Son of God. I pray for them. While I was with them in the world I kept them in Your name, and now I come to You and speak these things that they might have My joy fulfilled in themselves. As You have sent Me into the world, even so I have sent them into the world. And the glory which You gave Me, I have given them, that they may be one, even as We are one."

When He had finished praying He turned to His disciples and said, "I go to prepare a place for you. I will come again and receive you unto Myself, that where I am, there you may be also."

The disciples remembered the prayer and the promise of Jesus, and they held fast to it in hope. They knew that Jesus kept His promises. He would never fail His loved ones.

In the Garden
of Gethsemane

James and John were sometimes called the "fiery sons of thunder." Peter was the disciple who talked frequently of his loyalty to his Master. These three were the close friends of Jesus. Many times He chose them to be with Him for some great occasion.

The three friends knew of the love that Jesus had for them. They, too, loved Jesus, but their love was not great enough when it was put to test.

Jesus knew there were some sad days ahead. He wanted to go to some lonely place where He could talk to God, His Heavenly Father, and receive strength from Him. But Jesus wanted His dearest friends to be with Him at this time.

It was late at night. The disciples had celebrated the Passover Feast with Jesus in the upper room of Jerusalem. They left the quiet of that place and walked outside into the cool night air. They found their sandals lying side by side against the wall of the house. They put them on and followed Jesus.

He led the way through the narrow streets of Jerusalem and through the gate of the city. The little party crossed the Brook Kidron. Their path lay among the stone-walled orchards and gardens.

They walked together silently until they came to a small olive grove with a wall around it. It was called the garden of Gethsemane.

Jesus entered here and His disciples followed.

Eight of the disciples were told to wait. They settled themselves on the ground. They wrapped their cloaks about them to keep warm, for the night air was chilly. Soon they were fast asleep.

To Peter, James, and John, Jesus made a special request.

"I must pray to My Heavenly Father," He said. "Don't be far from Me. Stay near Me and watch."

The three disciples went forward with Jesus. They found a place near Him and settled themselves on the ground. Jesus had asked them to watch for Him.

But they failed their beloved Master. They closed their eyes. They cradled their heads in their arms and soon were fast asleep.

These three whom Jesus had chosen were surely no "sons of thunder" and loyal friends. They were sleepy companions who had failed their true Friend when He most needed their watchful care.

Meanwhile, Jesus prayed earnestly to God. After a time He left the place of prayer and walked over to His three disciples.

When He saw them sleeping, He said, "What! Could you not watch with Me for this short time? Remember, you must watch and pray always so that you may ever be true to Me."

Then Jesus returned to His lonely place. Again He poured out His soul in prayer. He was thinking of the terrible days that were to come. He needed strength from His Father in heaven.

A second time Jesus rose from the ground and hopefully walked toward His beloved friends. He wanted their sympathy and understanding love.

But they were fast asleep.

Slowly He walked away and returned to pray. He was so alone in this garden.

Huddled in a corner were His eight disciples, fast asleep. Nearby were His three close friends. They, too, were asleep. It seemed as though the very ones who were dearest to Him did not care enough to watch and wait with Him.

And there appeared to Jesus an angel from heaven, strengthening Him. God was with His beloved Son.

A third time Jesus rose from the ground. He was strong and ready to face all trials.

the
BETRAYAL

Into the garden of Gethsemane there came the sound of clattering of heels and loud voices. This quiet place that had been dark was now bright with the light of many torches.

The sleeping disciples rubbed their eyes. The noise had awakened them. The sudden light hurt their weary eyes. They rubbed them with their hands.

They were on their feet in a hurry. Here were enemies of Jesus coming to the garden. And they had been sleeping! They had failed to keep watch!

Peter quickly drew a sword from his belt and held it high. With this one sword he was bravely going to meet the enemy.

Jesus scolded him lightly and said, "Put up your sword. These things are to be. You cannot help now."

By the light of the torches, the disciples could see who had come to seize Jesus. There were servants of the chief Scribes and high priests, together with some soldiers who had been called to help. Heading this group was none other than Judas, who had been a disciple but who had hardened his heart against the beloved Master.

Jesus stepped forward and said, "Whom are you seeking?"

They answered Him, "Jesus of Nazareth.

"I am He," answered the Master.

The enemies were struck by the majesty of these words. They had come to capture Him, but instead they fell to the ground at His feet.

Then Jesus spoke to them, saying, "Why are you coming here to take Me? I was with you daily in the Temple, teaching, but you did not seize Me then.

"Do you think I cannot pray to My Father and He shall presently give Me more than twelve legions of angels to protect Me? But how then shall the Scriptures be fulfilled? It must be this way."

The disciples were filled with terror. With their ears they heard the brave words of Jesus, but their eyes beheld the swords which the enemies held in their hands. They were so frightened that every one of the eleven, fearful for his own life, ran away from the garden into the dark night.

They did not stay to hear the words of their beloved Master, who was even then begging mercy for them.

He asked nothing for Himself. But for His followers He asked, "Let these, my disciples, go their way."

Jesus was a faithful friend to those who had failed Him when He needed them most.

the trial
of jesus

The enemies of Jesus worked swiftly in the night. They knew they must carry out their plans before dawn, for in the bright and shining daylight there would be too many friends of Jesus to plead for Him.

These men were afraid of Jesus. They were afraid of the many followers who believed in Him and wanted to go His way. They knew only one way out. It was to be rid of Jesus.

Into the garden of Gethsemane these enemies sent their guards for Jesus. And He did not resist them.

Willingly, He went with the guards. Across the Brook Kidron they went. Through one of the eastern gates and up the slopes of the city they walked until they reached the palace of Caiaphas, the high priest. Here also lived Annas, another high priest. Any religious troubles of the people were brought to these two men.

Annas and Caiaphas were wicked leaders. They had been taking much money from the Temple in a dishonest way. Jesus had accused Annas of making the Temple a den of thieves instead of a place for worship. Here was his chance to punish Jesus for these words.

Jesus was brought before Annas in the middle of the night. The old priest was waiting for Him. He questioned the Saviour, hoping to receive some word from Him that could be used against Him.

Jesus only said, "I spoke openly to the world. I taught in the synagogues and in the Temple, where all could hear. I have said nothing in secret. Why, then, do you question Me at this time of night?"

Annas was furious. He did not like this answer. It was not what he expected. The old priest would have liked to question Jesus longer, but he knew there was not much time to waste. Jesus must be accused, tried, and condemned before daylight. He had to be delivered into the strong hands of the Roman government before morning, for if the friends of Jesus learned of this awful deed, they would be up in arms and rebel against these evil enemies.

Annas did not waste much time. He sent Jesus before Caiaphas, who was waiting in another part of the palace.

There were seventy men gathered in a circle around Caiaphas. They made a great show of dignity and honesty. Each man knew that Jesus was guilty of no wrong, but each wanted to accuse Him, because of the great fear and the awful pride in his own heart.

So the men talked among themselves about Jesus. What accusation could they make against Him? What crime could they say He had committed that would be punishable by death?

Jesus stood before His enemies. They were cross-legged on the floor, seated on cushions. Their heads were turbaned. They sat

like judges, but there was not a fair man among them. They looked at Jesus with hatred in their eyes, and their hearts were full of evil.

They waited for Jesus to speak. But He said nothing. He listened to their petty words.

At last Caiaphas became impatient. The time was growing short. The black night for evil plans was almost over.

He spoke sharply to Jesus. "I command You, by the living God, to tell us whether You are the Messiah, the Son of God!"

Jesus stood proudly before these enemies and said, "I am the Messiah, the Son of God!"

Caiaphas sprang from his seat. He stood dramatically before the assembled men. He tore his robe from his back.

"There now," he cried, "what more needs to be said? This Man claims He is the Son of God. He says He is a king! What will the Romans do when they hear this?"

There was an uproar among the assembled enemies of Jesus. They took His words and twisted them around to their own evil use.

Swiftly the guards were ordered to send Jesus to the palace of Pilate, the Roman leader and governor. Pilate would not dare free Jesus if this group of leaders sent a message saying they had a prisoner who was trying to be king of the land.

So it was that Jesus was taken before Pilate, the Roman governor, falsely accused of wanting to be an earthly king.

Jesus was the Son of God. He did talk of a kingdom, but it was not an earthly place. Jesus was thinking of an everlasting kingdom in heaven.

It was a night when black plans were carried out by wicked men. The enemies of Jesus were afraid. In their fear they thought only of themselves.

They could not understand Jesus when He told them of the kingdom in heaven where there was love for God and love for one another.

Jesus
Before Pilate

In the early morning hours Jesus was brought before Pilate, the governor. He was tried in the open air, in the courtyard of the palace.

Pilate wanted to be fair. He did not want any harm to come to Jesus. The governor listened to the accusations made against the Saviour.

Pilate said to the enemies, "I find no fault in Jesus."

But the wicked men would not listen to such a verdict. They frightened Pilate by saying, "Whoever makes himself a king is speaking against Caesar."

Pilate was afraid of Caesar, for he was the ruler over all the land. But the governor did not want to harm Jesus. So he sent him to another leader named Herod. But Herod returned Jesus to Pilate.

Again the governor stood before the angry enemies of Jesus.

He said, "What shall I do with Jesus?"

With evil hearts, they cried loudly, "Crucify Him! Crucify Him!"

Pilate could not let this happen to the Saviour, whom he knew was innocent of any wrong.

"I will not crucify Him," he cried. "I will scourge Him and let Him go!"

Jesus was led away. He was brutally beaten. With horrible mockery, a wreath of thorns was put on His head in place of a crown. A purple cloak was thrown over His bleeding shoulders. And Jesus was brought once again to Pilate, amidst the wild cries of His tormentors.

Pilate was afraid. The angry people who stood before him could do him great harm. He was afraid of them. But Jesus had said He was the Son of God. And Pilate was afraid of Jesus.

He looked at Jesus and said, "Don't You know that I have the power to crucify or release You?"

Jesus said, "You would have no power against Me unless it was given to you from above. You are bad, but those who have delivered Me to you have committed a greater sin than yours."

Pilate stood before the waiting, angry people. He washed his hands and said, "I am innocent of the blood of this righteous Man. Do what you will with Him."

The enemies of Jesus cried, "His blood be on us and on our children!"

So Jesus was led away to be crucified. His enemies had used the dark night to carry out their evil plans.

Jesus did not call upon God for help. He knew there were many who loved Him and believed in Him. He was willing to suffer for them.

The angry, frightened enemies who crowded around Him were few in number, compared to the many followers of Jesus.

the crucifixion

It was the middle of the day, when the sun shines brightest. But on this day there was something wrong. The sky was blacker than it was in the middle of the night!

The earth began to shake and tremble. Rocks which had been solid in the ground began to roll and turn like small pebbles.

Jesus was dying on the cross and all heaven was sorrowing. In fierce anguish He suffered, but a veil of darkness covered Him so that none might see His awful agony.

Jesus hung on the cross and suffered great bodily pain, and His soul was sorrowing, for He bore the sins of the people of the world.

Drop by drop, His blood spilled from the cross where He hung. They had pierced His hands and His feet with great nails. They had crowned Him with a crown of thorns. And He suffered willingly for all who believed in Him. He loved others more than He did Himself. His love was so great that He gave His life for them.

There was no bitterness in His heart for those who had caused this terrible thing to happen.

The first words which Jesus said, after they hung Him on the cross, were words of pity. He looked about Him at the enemies who stood nearby. He thought about Annas and Caiaphas, the high priests, and the other enemies who had said He must die.

As a great priest, Jesus came before God His Father and asked forgiveness for His enemies.

As He hung on the cross, He looked toward heaven and prayed, "Father, forgive them, for they know not what they do."

Now, there were two thieves who had been hung on crosses near Jesus. The one thief mocked and jeered at Him. But the other one cried, "Have you no fear of God? We are dying be-

cause we deserve this punishment, but this Man has done nothing wrong. It is no time to mock, when we are so near death."

The thief then spoke to Jesus and said, "O Lord, remember me when You enter into Your kingdom."

As a mighty king, Jesus answered the thief, "This very day you shall be with Me in paradise!"

The time dragged on. The suffering of Jesus became greater and greater. Even in His awful agony, He thought of those whom He loved. He wanted to help them, for He knew they were sorrowing because of Him.

He heard the weeping of women who stood near the cross. His own mother, Mary, was with these women, and in great love and pity He looked down upon her. He sorrowed that she should see Him at this time.

The beloved disciple John was standing nearby, trying to comfort Mary.

Jesus wanted to provide a home for His mother. And He wanted to honor this truly beloved disciple, who had proved himself to be so faithful.

"Behold, here is John," Jesus said to His mother. "Let him be as a son to you, to take My place."

And looking to John, Jesus said, "To you, I give My mother; let her be your mother, for My sake."

From that time, John took Mary into his home and treated her with loving care as he would his own beloved parent.

There was a great silence. For three long hours Jesus suffered horrible pain. Not one word did He utter. And in that time the whole earth mourned. The sky was black. The land trembled and shook.

The enemies of Jesus tried to find their way around in the dark. They did not know what to do. They were afraid. They wanted to hide.

They remembered the words they had cried not many hours before: "Let the blood of Jesus be on our heads!"

They had bravely cried the words to Pilate. That was when they wanted to crucify Jesus. That was when they nailed Him to the cross, and before the very heavens and earth showed displeasure at the awful thing which had been done.

Now, those who had mockingly called Him Jesus the king gravely admitted, "Surely Jesus was the Son of God."

There were those who remembered that He had said, "Do you think I cannot pray to My Father and He shall give Me more than twelve legions of angels to protect Me?"

Jesus was strong and mighty! He was the Son of God!

Everyone mourned. The enemies, who had hurt Him, were afraid for what they had done. The friends of Jesus were sad because of the bitter suffering their beloved Master had to endure. And they wanted Jesus with them. They were as sheep without a shepherd. They forgot the promise He made. He said He would be with them in a little while, but in their sorrow they forgot His words of promise.

It was midafternoon. Three hours of agony had slowly passed by. They were hours of terrifying silence.

The silence was broken.

There was a great cry.

Those who were near the cross heard the last words that Jesus said, triumphantly: "It is finished!"

His bitter suffering was over. In great agony He had hung on the cross. He had given His life for His loved ones. The great work of salvation was now, at last, completed.

Gently, Jesus uttered the last words to His Father in heaven, saying, "Father, into Thy hands I commend My spirit."

In that moment a great and terrible thing happened at the Temple in Jerusalem.

In the Temple there hung a huge curtain of purple and gold that separated the Holy of Holies from the eyes of the congregation. Only at certain times could special priests go beyond this curtain, into the Holy Place.

At the very moment when Jesus spoke His last words to God in heaven, the great curtain suddenly split in two, from top to bottom. There, before the eyes of all, was the Holy of Holies, no longer sanctified. It was revealed for all to see.

In terror, the enemies of Jesus said, "Truly, He was the Son of God!"

In great awe the friends of Jesus beheld the strange happenings of the day. When they saw the darkened sky and the trembling earth, their faith became stronger. When they heard about the torn curtain in the Temple, they knew that Jesus was the Son of God.

Friends and enemies alike bowed down in great awe. In their hearts, they knew that Jesus, who had lived among them, blameless and without sin, was indeed the Son of God!

the
watchful guard

It was early morning. Through the gray shadows of the dawn, the dim outline of a great stone could be seen. It was placed before a tomb.

Soldiers marched back and forth in front of it. The king's seal was placed on the tomb to prevent anyone from moving the great stone.

This was the tomb that belonged to Joseph of Arimathaea. Jesus lay buried within its sealed doors.

Surely the enemies of Jesus had nothing to fear now. They had crucified Him. They had pierced His side to be certain He was dead. He was locked within the tomb and a guard was on constant watch outside. But still they were frightened.

They could not forget the awful signs from God which they had seen with their own eyes. The bright noon sky had become black as night while Jesus hung on the cross. The very earth had trembled. At the moment when Jesus died, the great curtain of the Temple had been torn in two, revealing the Holy of Holies.

Jesus was the Son of God. And God in heaven had shown His wrath for the awful deed that had been done.

Jesus had told His enemies, "In three days I shall rise again." And they were frightened!

Every precaution was taken so that Jesus could not leave the tomb. Strong soldiers were on guard. They carried sharp swords for protection.

Jesus' enemies hoped that now they would have no more trouble. They did not consider that strong men are weak against the power of God.

So the soldiers kept their watch in the early dawn. A feeble fire glowed nearby for them to warm themselves, as it was cool. The fire also served as a light to see if anyone approached.

It was almost time to change watch. More guards would soon come to relieve these men from their vigil. The hours had dragged through the night. The soldiers were anxious to leave the tomb and return to the city.

Suddenly the earth began to tremble under their feet. The soldiers drew their swords, ready for trouble. But their strong arms and mighty weapons were of no use against the power of God.

A mighty angel of the Lord descended from heaven and rolled back the stone from the tomb and sat upon it. His face was like lightning and the garments he wore were as white as snow.

The guards shook with fear. They fell to the ground and lay there as if they were dead.

Jesus came forth from the tomb. He had risen from the dead. All the power of men on earth could not prevail against Him!

the empty tomb

It was early in the morning. Some women walked along the road. Their steps were slow and lagging. They were grief-stricken. Their eyes were red from weeping. In their hands they carried sweet perfumes.

These were faithful friends of Jesus. They were on the way to the tomb where Jesus lay. They wanted to anoint His body with the perfume and perform the last rites of burial, according to the custom of those days.

As the women walked along, they talked about a problem that had come to mind.

"Who shall roll away the stone from the door of the tomb?" they pondered.

The women were not strong enough to move the great stone, for it weighed many pounds. They wondered if the guards would help. And the guards had to be willing to let them enter the tomb. All of these things must be considered before they were able to attend to their beloved Jesus.

When they reached the tomb, they saw that the great stone had been rolled away. The guards were gone. The women were free to enter!

They could not understand this strange turn of events. They knew that the king's seal had been placed on the tomb. They also knew that soldiers had been on constant guard before the tomb. What, then, had happened?

Timidly the women approached the tomb. They were almost afraid to look inside.

They stepped a little closer. They went inside the tomb. The body of Jesus was not there! It was gone!

The linen wrappings lay on the bier, exactly as they had been wound about His body. The napkin that was tied around His head was there, but Jesus was gone!

The women looked up. They saw an angel in shining white, waiting as if to tell them some good news. And there was a second angel before them, too!

The women bowed their faces to the earth in great awe and wonder. These strange happenings were signs from heaven!

Then the angel told the glorious news.

"Fear not," said he, "for I know you are seeking Jesus who was crucified. Why do you look for the living among the dead? He is not here, for He is risen! Behold the place where they laid Him. It is empty. But go, quickly. Tell Peter and the other disciples that He is risen from the dead!"

The women fled from the tomb. They hurried to give the message to the friends of Jesus. They did not stop to tell the news to anyone they met along the way.

Mary of Magdala was one of the women. She hurried to the home where Peter and John were staying. Quickly she told them all the strange events that had happened at the tomb of Jesus.

Peter and John could scarcely believe her words. They wanted to see for themselves whether the tomb was empty.

The two disciples raced from the house and ran as swiftly as their legs would take them. John was younger than Peter, and he reached the tomb first.

When John came to the open door and saw the great stone rolled away, he did not enter. He was content to peer inside.

Peter came running to the tomb. He was not timid like John. He hurried inside and looked about him.

He saw the linen wrappings and the folded napkin in their places. Even the spices which had been placed within the folds of the wrappings were there.

Peter and John walked out of the tomb. They hastened to town. They had wonderful tidings to tell.

Jesus had risen from the dead!

Now, Mary of Magdala had delivered the message as the angel had told her, but she was not satisfied. She wanted to know more about her Master.

Slowly she returned along the road she had taken earlier that morning. Again she stood before the tomb where Jesus had lain.

At the door of the empty tomb she stood weeping. Mary wanted to find her Master.

At last she stooped down and looked into the tomb. She saw two angels in bright robes, one sitting at the head and one at the foot of the place where the body of Jesus had lain.

"Woman," said one of the angels, "why do you weep?"

Tearfully, Mary answered, "They have taken away my Lord, and I do not know where they have laid Him."

Still weeping, Mary turned from the tomb and started to walk away.

She looked up. A man stood before her.

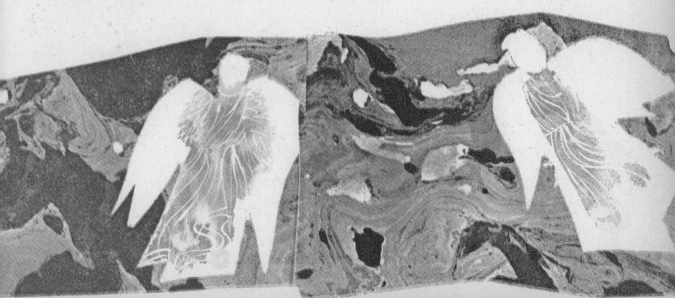

"Why do you weep?" asked the stranger.

Mary did not know this man. She thought he might be a gardener who worked there. Perhaps he could tell her where to find Jesus.

"Sir," Mary said, "if you have carried Jesus from the tomb, please tell me where you have laid Him and I will take Him away."

There was no reply to her question. Then she heard her name spoken, and the voice was one that Mary knew and loved.

It was Jesus who spoke gently to her, saying, "Mary!"

The stranger who stood before her was not the gardener! Mary was looking into the face of Jesus, her beloved Master.

He had risen from the dead! He stood now, before her. And the tears of grief that stained her cheeks were now glistening teardrops of joy.

"Master," cried Mary of Magdala.

"Do not touch Me," said Jesus, "I have not yet ascended to My Father in heaven. But go to My disciples and tell them that I ascend to My God and your God."

Joyfully, Mary hurried to the disciples with the news.

"I have seen the Lord! Jesus has risen from the dead!"

the RISEN LORD

Ten disciples of Jesus were gathered together secretly, behind closed doors. Thomas, who belonged to their number, was not there.

Excitedly they talked about the great happenings of the day. Each man present wanted to have a part in the conversation.

"Jesus has risen from the dead!" exclaimed Peter. "Mary of Magdala told us to go to the tomb. We ran there."

"I was there first," said John. "I looked in and Jesus was not there."

"The grave clothes were left untouched," cried Peter. "I went inside and looked closely. It was as if Jesus had slipped out of them. They had not been unwound. Even the spices were within the folds."

"It was Mary of Magdala who saw Jesus first," said one of the disciples. "She did not know Him, but when He spoke her name and she looked again, He appeared to her as the risen Lord."

"I saw Him, too," said Peter. "Just this afternoon He suddenly appeared to me and talked to me."

"It is too wonderful!" exclaimed another disciple. "Just think how sad we were. We were like sheep without a shepherd. Our

Master was gone from us. We did not know where to turn or what was to become of us."

"We were so sad that we completely forgot the promise Jesus made to us. He said He would be gone for only a little while and then He would return," said a third disciple.

Someone else started to speak, but there was a knock on the door. A disciple opened the door and two men rushed inside.

"We have news for you! We have seen the Lord," said one man. "We hurried to tell you about it."

"Yes," added the other man, who was named Cleopas. "We were on our way to Emmaus, our home, when a stranger over-took us. We did not know him."

"We were talking about Jesus," said the first man. "The stranger listened to us closely. He asked us questions."

"Then he quoted Scripture to us," said Cleopas, "as one who knew it well. Through words of prophesy that are in God's Book, he told about the death of Jesus and His resurrection. And we wondered who this man was."

The visitor did not want to leave any part of the story untold.

He said, "We climbed the hill path together through the terraces of vines and olives, and when we entered into the village gate the stranger said good-bye to us."

"But we asked him to come to our house, and he did," explained Cleopas. "We offered him a simple meal, and when He blessed it we knew in that moment that this was no stranger. We had been with Jesus."

The disciples and their friends talked about the wonder of the risen Lord. The room was closed from all outsiders. The door was fastened securely.

Suddenly the very One about whom they had been talking appeared in their presence.

"Peace be unto you," said Jesus.

The disciples and friends were frightened. They could not believe their own eyes.

"Why are you troubled?" asked Jesus. "Look at My hands and My feet. See the prints of the nails there. Now you know that it is I, your Saviour."

The disciples were filled with unspeakable joy. Jesus, their Saviour, was in their midst. No longer did they feel like sheep without a shepherd.

Jesus spoke to His beloved friends.

"You can understand now why I did not come to the world to rule an earthly kingdom. God sent Me to the world to help His people, whom He loves. In the Scriptures you will find it says that the Messiah had to shed His blood for the sins of the people, and on the third day He should rise again from the dead. All this has been fulfilled and now at last, you, My friends, can understand these things."

The wondering disciples listened to their beloved Master.

"Peace be unto you," said Jesus. "As My Father has sent Me, even so send I you."

Then Jesus was gone from among them. As suddenly as He had appeared to them, so He left them, in the locked room.

But their hearts were no longer troubled. They had seen the risen Lord. He had given them a task to do. They were to go out into the world and tell others about Jesus, who had died for their sins and had risen from the dead in order to establish a kingdom in heaven for His loved ones.

DOUBTING THOMAS

There was a disciple called Thomas. But there was added to his name another word and he was known by it throughout the years.

They called him Doubting Thomas because he always wanted to be sure about everything before he had a part in it. He was the one who said "How?" and "Why?"

Thomas said, "I have to be shown before I can believe."

When the other ten disciples came to Thomas and told him the amazing news that they had seen Jesus, he doubted them.

He said, "Unless I see the print of the nails in His hands and can put my finger into the print of the nails and thrust my hand into His side where the sword pierced, I will not believe!"

Eight days passed by. The ten disciples still talked of the wonder of seeing Jesus, who had risen from the dead. Doubting Thomas listened to their talk, but he did not believe what they said.

Again they were gathered in a room with many other friends. The door was closed against outsiders.

Suddenly, Jesus appeared before them. Again He said the familiar words of greeting, "Peace be unto you."

Then Jesus walked directly toward His doubting disciple. He repeated the very words of doubt that Thomas had spoken to the ten disciples.

Jesus said, "Reach out and touch My hand. Feel the scar from the nail that was driven into it when they crucified Me. Reach out and touch My side where the sword was thrust into it. Be not faithless, Thomas, but believing."

Thomas fell at the feet of Jesus. He knew that his beloved Master stood before him. He was awed that Jesus should repeat the very words of doubt that he had spoken to the disciples. Surely here was Jesus, the glorified Messiah, who had triumphed over death and stood a living proof before his very eyes.

The faith of Thomas was made strong. From that time forward, he always believed in Jesus. Thomas resolved to go forth and tell many others about Jesus, the Son of God, whom he had seen risen from the dead!

Thomas worshiped Jesus and said, "My Lord and my God."

"Thomas," said Jesus, "because you have seen Me, you have believed. Blessed are they that have not seen and yet have believed!"

The Saviour was thinking ahead to the many years to come, when the story of Jesus would be told and those who heard it would believe. They would not be doubters, like Doubting Thomas, who had to see before he believed!

jesus helps
his loved ones

Peter stood looking out upon the rippling waters of the sea.

He turned to some of the disciples who were with him and said, "Just look at the Sea of Galilee! What happy memories come back when I look out upon her waters. We were fishermen here when Jesus called us to leave our nets and follow Him."

"Will you ever forget the times He saved our lives when we were in those violent storms?" said one of the disciples.

"He had only to speak to the wind and the waves and they obeyed Him," said another disciple. "Much has happened since then. Three years have passed and we have been with Jesus all that time."

"He said once that we would meet Him here," said John. "Perhaps He will come soon."

Peter continued looking out upon the sea. He had been a fisherman for many years. He felt the old desire to cast his net into the waters and bring up a good catch of fish.

"I'm going to fish," said he.

"We shall go with you," said the other disciples, and they all entered a boat and set out to sea.

At first the hours passed by swiftly. Each time the net was

215

thrown over the side of the boat and into the sea, there was hope that when the men pulled it up it would be full of fish.

And they tried, time after time, these disciples of Jesus, who were now fishing in the Sea of Galilee. But they did not bring up any fish. Their net was always empty. They moved from one place to another, hoping each time to find a spot where they could catch some fish.

All night long they cast their net into the sea, but not one fish was caught.

As the morning light was beginning to break, the fishermen found themselves not very far from land. Their eyes were not turned toward the shore, for they were too busy with their net.

They did not see a stranger standing on the beach watching them. They did not know that anyone was near at this early hour, until they heard a voice.

"Children, have you any meat?" called the stranger.

Very kindly he spoke to them. He spoke as a father asking his own children about their needs so that he could provide for them.

But the fishermen were too busy to bother with the stranger.

Their answer was short. Without even looking toward shore, the men replied, "No, we have caught nothing."

They continued throwing the net into the water, only to pull it out empty each time.

Again the stranger called to them.

"Cast your net on the right side of the ship," he said. "You shall find fish there."

The net was cast over the right side of the boat. This time

when all hands pulled at the net to bring it up from the sea it was so heavy with fish that the disciples could scarcely lift it. Each man pulled and strained, using all his strength.

Up and up they pulled, but even when every man strained and pulled with all his might, the net could not be dragged over the side and into the boat.

The fishermen looked down. Their net was filled with wriggling, jumping fish. They were like flashes of silver, as they bobbed and squirmed in the net. And the net was whole! With all the strain of the great catch, it had not torn. This was a miracle! And the stranger, on the shore, had caused it to happen.

This man was no stranger to the disciples.

"It is the Lord!" cried John.

Peter could not wait to row the boat to shore. He wanted to hurry to Jesus. Fastening his fisher's coat about him, he cast himself into the water and swam toward Jesus.

The other men were anxious to see their Master. They swiftly rowed their boat to shore, dragging alongside the net filled with fish.

At last they reached the shore. Quickly they left the boat and ran toward Jesus.

They stood beside Him shivering because they were cold and wet. They were hungry, too, after the long night's work.

There came the sound of a crackling fire. There was the smell of frying fish. What had Jesus done for His disciples?

He had known they were cold and weary. He knew they were hungry. Jesus had made this fire to warm them and He had prepared a meal to satisfy their hunger.

"Bring the fish which you have caught," said Jesus.

It was Peter who finally brought the net to shore. When they were counted, there were one hundred and fifty-three fish in this one great haul. Yet, with all the weight, the net was not broken!

"Come and dine," said Jesus, and He served His friends in the early morning, by the Sea of Galilee.

The seven fishermen had gone fishing, but with all their efforts they had failed to make a catch.

With the appearance of Jesus, all was changed. The net was filled with fish. And when the men came ashore, cold and hungry, Jesus was there waiting for them with food and a warm fire.

Jesus was there when they needed Him most, just as He is close at hand to help His loved ones who need Him today and every other day.

the ascension

The time had come for Jesus to return to heaven and be with God His Father.

As a tiny babe He came to the earth, and the angels sang, "Glory to God in the highest, and on earth peace, goodwill toward men!"

As a child, Jesus listened and learned about God's Holy Book. His mother, Mary, and Joseph were His teachers in their home, and He was a good scholar in the synagogue school.

When Jesus was a young man and fully prepared to do the work for which He had been sent, God spoke from heaven and said, "This is My beloved Son, in whom I am well pleased."

From that time on, Jesus spent His life helping others. He told about the great love of His Heavenly Father. He was, at all times, doing the work God had sent Him to do on earth.

In all His life, He did not sin.

When the time came, Jesus willingly gave His own life that those who believed in Him should have life everlasting in heaven.

Jesus died on the cross. His body was carried away by loving friends and placed in a tomb. But Jesus did not stay in the tomb where He had been placed.

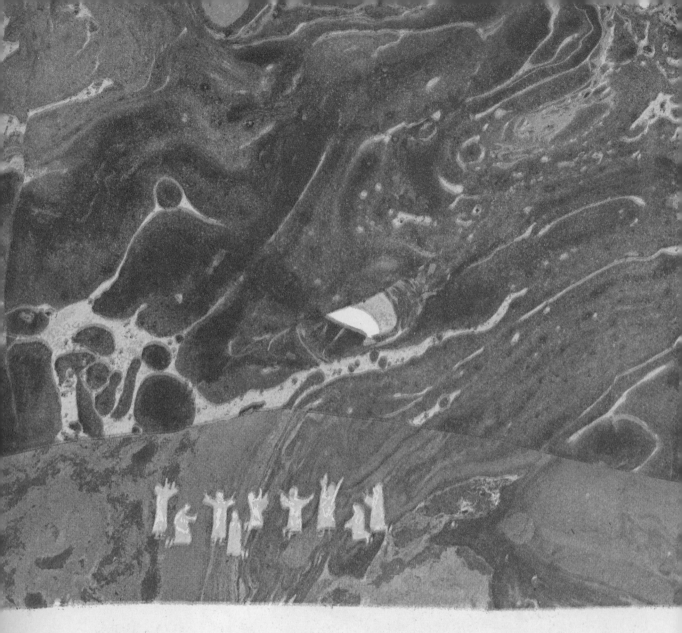

Jesus rose from the dead!

He appeared to those who loved Him and were His faithful followers. Many times He came to them. He appeared suddenly before them, when they did not expect Him. He talked to them.

When forty days had passed, it was time for Jesus to return to heaven. His work on earth was finished.

The beloved disciples of Jesus were ready to carry on the work that He had begun.

Jesus told them, "Go and teach all nations, baptizing them in the name of the Father, and of the Son, and of the Holy Ghost, teaching them to observe all things whatsoever I have commanded you. And lo, I am with you always, even unto the end of the world."

Jesus gave them a promise.

He said, "The Comforter, which is the Holy Ghost, whom the Father will send in My name, He shall teach you all things and bring all things to your remembrance, whatsoever I have said unto you. Peace I leave with you. My peace I give unto you."

So Jesus led His beloved friends along the road to Bethany until they came to a place on the Mount of Olives.

Jesus lifted up His hands and blessed His friends. And while He was blessing them, He was parted from them. He was taken up into heaven and a cloud received Him out of their sight.

While they looked earnestly into the heavens, two angels in white stood by the faithful friends and said, "Why are you looking up to heaven? This same Jesus which is taken up to heaven shall come again as you have seen Him go."

The faithful followers of Jesus rejoiced as they witnessed Jesus ascending into heaven.

They were reminded of the Psalm of David:

"Lift up your heads, O ye gates; and be ye lifted up, ye everlasting doors; and the King of Glory shall come in!"

Jesus, their Redeemer, lived! He would reign forever in heaven.

The Whitman
Library of
Giant Books

FAVORITE STORIES
A collection of the
best-loved tales of
childhood, illustrated
by Don Bolognese, Betty
Fraser, Kelly Oechsli

THE MERRY MOTHER GOOSE
Over 450 Mother Goose
Rhymes, illustrated by
Ruth Ruhman

THE MAGIC REALM OF
FAIRY TALES
Classic fairy tales,
illustrated by Leslie
Gray, Judy Stang

STORIES OF JESUS
Told by Thea Heinemann,
with illustrations by
Don Bolognese

ANIMAL STORIES
By William Johnston,
with illustrations by
Frank Aloise, June
Goldsborough

365 BEDTIME STORIES
By Nan Gilbert,
with illustrations by
Bill McKibbin